MW00939268

The Conqueress

A Guide to Overcoming Obstacles and Honoring Yourself

DR. MARCY BUEHLER

BALBOA.PRESS

A DIVISION OF HAY HOUSE

Copyright © 2021 Dr. Marcy Buehler.

All rights reserved. No part of this book may be used or reproduced by any means, graphic, electronic, or mechanical, including photocopying, recording, taping or by any information storage retrieval system without the written permission of the author except in the case of brief quotations embodied in critical articles and reviews.

Balboa Press books may be ordered through booksellers or by contacting:

Balboa Press
A Division of Hay House
1663 Liberty Drive
Bloomington, IN 47403
www.balboapress.com
844-682-1282

Because of the dynamic nature of the Internet, any web addresses or links contained in this book may have changed since publication and may no longer be valid. The views expressed in this work are solely those of the author and do not necessarily reflect the views of the publisher, and the publisher hereby disclaims any responsibility for them.

The author of this book does not dispense medical advice or prescribe the use of any technique as a form of treatment for physical, emotional, or medical problems without the advice of a physician, either directly or indirectly. The intent of the author is only to offer information of a general nature to help you in your quest for emotional and spiritual well-being. In the event you use any of the information in this book for yourself, which is your constitutional right, the author and the publisher assume no responsibility for your actions.

Print information available on the last page.

ISBN: 978-1-9822-6743-8 (sc)
ISBN: 978-1-9822-6800-8 (hc)
ISBN: 978-1-9822-6742-1 (e)

Balboa Press rev. date: 04/30/2021

For Every Soul that Longs to be Known.

Contents

Preface ix

Introduction xvii

The Conqueress 1

The Problem 2

The Four Shifts

Physical Shift 11

Psychological Shift 18

Social Shift 21

Spiritual Shift 24

The Value of Support 28

Layer 1: Feel 34

Layer 2: Explore 53

Layer 3: Acceptance 80

Layer 4: Transform 103

The Unfolding 125

References 133

Acknowledgements 137

About the Author 139

Preface

It was the first time I had naysayers: people who truly cared about me but now questioned my ideas and challenged my decisions without my solicitation. I had never been one to heed the opinions of others when my decision had already been made. Rather, I was governed by a strong-willed mindset. I was going to do what I had set out to do. I was the teenager who got her bellybutton pierced without parental consent. The child who decided to go to college with little input from the adults in my life. The small-town girl who announced I was moving across the country. The Catholic girl who declared I was moving in with my boyfriend. I was the girl who was going to learn lessons the hard way, the one who needed real experiences to make decisions and learn for myself.

My parents came to accept that I was going to make my own decisions and they rarely tried to intervene. It had become part of my identity as the oldest daughter of five children. I took responsibility for myself and navigated much of my life with minimal guidance or support. And, for the most part, at least from an outside perspective, I had done okay, so they let me be. But even during those bold actions, I had always felt small, judged, and insecure, running from something or trying to hide and go unnoticed.

The Fall

This isolation and the illusion of success followed me into adulthood. After migrating to the West Coast with my then boyfriend, we built a home in the suburbs and ran a profitable business. I was dependent on no one and free from having to nurture and please others. This solitude gave me some peace. Our business thrived. The financial abundance was novel to both he and I. I had been raised on a farm; we were taught to conserve and be thrifty. He had a similar history in a family of nine children. Financial abundance and the constant pursuit of success kept me occupied. And numb.

That storybook life didn't last long. Our eleven-year relationship turned 180 degrees and life as I had known it was gone. We lost our business, our dream home, and the brand-new silver Jeep Grand Cherokee Limited Edition with a sunroof and leather interior that I had paid for with cash at the naive age of 27. The divorce and the custody battles lasted three agonizing years. During that time, we never spoke outside of court while I had sole custody of our young daughter. My nearest family lived nearly two thousand miles away; it was humbling to ask them for help after having become a grown, self-sufficient woman. My dream of being a stay-at-home mother became a resented desire. I was now responsible financially, emotionally, and physically for providing for myself and my daughter. I was angry at all the other divorcees who got direct-deposit checks in their accounts each month from their ex-husbands. I resented the single moms I was trying to befriend who would pop into the gym in their new Lululemon workout clothes. Their biggest dilemma seemed to be how much Botox would remove the wrinkles and still allow them to raise their eyebrows when needed. All this while they stayed at home enjoying alimony and child support. I went through many moments of grief and torment.

On top of all that, I was in constant fear of my ex-husband's delusional state. The man of my dreams, who I wanted to believe could change, had suddenly become a complete stranger. That was the hardest part to deal with – perhaps even harder than death. I would look at this man, all six foot, three inches of him with his pearly white smile, gorgeous blue eyes, and charismatic demeanor, and wonder where he went. Staring at his dilated pupils and listening to his irrational thoughts would open a pit in my stomach. The man I married would not have made me tremble in fear or make such accusations. Prior to that, he had adored and respected me; he placed me on a pedestal. To this day, I can honestly say that he has one of the most beautiful souls I have ever known. Yet at its culmination, the unresolved trauma and prescription medications had taken possession of him and changed him. My heart broke into a million pieces, the future I envisioned completely pulled out from under me.

I remember desperately trying to control him and wanting to make him stop. I thought I knew the solutions to fix him or at least make things better. I now understand that my enabling wasn't helpful and likely prolonged his journey to wellness. He was never mine to fix. Hiding the realities behind closed doors and covering up for irrational behaviors only brought more shame and harder falls. I realized I had been operating from a distorted belief system in which hiding the truths equated to loyalty and martyrdom was honorable. Pulling the truth out of the shadows and into the light allowed me to see things for what they were rather than the distorted illusions that I longed for.

The chaos and rapid, intense fall of our marriage also impacted our livelihood. We were entrepreneurs and had accomplished much. Yet the combination of his condition and a crash in the real estate market took everything from us. I was grateful that at least I had an education. Prior to this upheaval, I had gotten a master's degree with the intent of becoming a school psychologist. However, working for myself was far more lucrative and allowed me the luxury of creating my own schedule. Beneath that was also relief – a reprieve from a deep fear of failure, of having to perform on my own. With the business, I could hide in the shadows of my husband. I didn't have to be seen or heard; I worked behind the scenes while he ran the show.

Now in this vulnerable position, I found myself having to show up. It wasn't an option; my daughter and I would survive, even if it meant stepping outside my comfort level. With tenacity and some newly opened doors, I applied for a position in the school district where I lived and was immediately offered the job. I had only finished my program two years earlier and never worked in the field, making this internship full of learning and challenges. The responsibility of having to financially provide for and physically care for myself and daughter weighed heavily on me.

If that wasn't enough, I was still dealing with my ex-husband in a situation I had little clarity about. He knew how to push my buttons. He knew that my daughter was the most important person in my life and that I would go to any lengths to defend her. He also knew that questioning my ability as a mother was the biggest dagger to my heart. Coming from the person I thought loved me the most, the man I had planned to spend my life with, who had fathered this being, made me question myself and my worth on a regular basis.

In addition to the emotional pain, physical exhaustion and guilt began to pile up. I remember rushing from work to pick up my daughter from daycare because I felt so guilty being away from her. There was no "me" time or time for the self-care and healing that I so desperately needed. All I wanted to do was numb out. Yet I had to stay strong, be on top of my game, because every action and every word were dissected in hopes of using them against me in court and sabotaging my relationship with my daughter. I'll never forget the bitterness of his words: "If I'm going down, I'm taking you with me." More importantly, I'll never forget how those words propelled me into an armor of protection and self-preservation.

I still look back on all this with a deep sense of sadness. It was not the experience I had thought it would be. I had imagined us walking together in the park with the baby stroller, summers at the beach, game nights, and warm, cozy family holidays. Instead, my holidays became bittersweet reminders of unmet dreams.

The Conqueress

In my struggles, I discovered a fierce self-love and made a commitment to myself that I would never ever allow someone to take me or my daughter down. I began to see how much of my identity and security had been rooted in my marriage and in another human being. I had allowed my worth to be defined by others which had robbed myself of being me. I now had clarity on why I hid in the shadows so that I wouldn't have to be known, judged, or wrong. My worth, my goals, my opinions, and my thoughts had been meticulously orchestrated to please and appease others. My body, mind, and soul, although residing in the same home, had become strangers. This was far from the image I wanted to model for my daughter, nor the path I wanted to stay on for me.

Unbeknownst to others, a flame within me ignited. Applying for my doctoral program during this dark period raised a few eyebrows. From an outside perspective, there was very little logic to this decision due to the time and financial constraints as well as the dedication it would take to complete my dissertation. Yet I had always been highly intuitive with a strong spiritual connection. Religion came and went, but my spiritual connection was constant. Even in the darkness, I remember praying through my tears, asking God, *Why is this mine to endure?* I pleaded that my suffering not be in vain, that somehow it would benefit others. I prayed that my healing journey would serve as a testimony and a beacon of hope. I had witnessed so much suffering in so many others through both my profession and my healing journey. I wasn't alone and I knew it didn't have to be this way. Intuitively, I knew I needed to enroll in this doctoral program. I needed to learn new skills that I could apply to my own life in order to heal and re-establish the intimate connection I desired between my mind, body, and soul. Once I had healed, I could then help others to heal.

I identified this intense inner force as "The Conqueress." She represents my highest, best version of myself, the being I was always meant to be. She is the inter-woven manifestation of mind, body, and soul. Within the Conqueress resides our ancestral wisdom, absolute and pure love, and the pursuit to align with our purpose. I have come to believe that this determined and tenacious force exists within us all, though through our evolutions and revolutions, it somehow became buried, shamed, and afraid – yet always yearning to return out of the shadows. Because my situation had brought me to a point of desperation and determination, the Conqueress could no longer be still. That fierce warrior-like self-love woke up within me and was ready to serve and heal. She would defend and protect me from the internal and external forces that sought to make me less. She was ready to be free. She was ready to be seen. She was ready to be heard and to be fully known. She was ready to rise above my circumstance with both grace and grit.

Even when I shrugged off her strengthening voice, she kept nudging me with subtle signs. In my prayer and meditation, I started to see the unfolding. I knew this was my path, the way for me to survive and thrive. When I recognized that I would have to live with the consequences of my decisions, good or bad, I stopped caring so much about pleasing others or what they thought. Now a mom, I was responsible for a child as well. I wanted to model strength, grace, and perseverance. I wanted her to see her mother as an intelligent, compassionate, and beautiful woman who honored and respected herself. I wanted to demonstrate healthy boundaries by showing her what I will and will not stand for in the most compassionate and firm manner. I wanted her to discover her unique and authentic self and know that my love had no boundaries. I shrugged off the naysayers and applied for the doctoral program, allowing the intuitive voice of the Conqueress to guide the course of my life.

It's Your Time

Initially, I wanted to write a book because I had a story to tell. Along the way, I found that it wasn't my story, however traumatic or personal, that was so unique but what I had come to find as a solution. There are many stories like mine, so much insecurity, fear, and emotional pain that needlessly persist. Having lived through that story and finding a path out, I discovered a passion and a determination to offer hope and show others that there is a better way.

For a long while as I wrote, I debated just how much of my soul I would bare; I didn't want to risk hurting others and unveil truths that long lived in the shadows. But then I realized that's what I've done for most of my life. I've sacrificed my truth, my thoughts, and my beliefs to preserve a false sense of peace. As a result, I jeopardized my self-integrity and compromised my self-worth. No more. This is my time. This is my truth. This is my story. This is my song. And now it will be yours. Your healing journey will be your time, your truth, your story, your song. Let go of the messages, standards, and opinions of others. There is no other choice.

Further, as I work with clients, I am continually reminded that we've all been conditioned to become the people we are as a result of our experiences and upbringing. This includes our parents and family, who likely did the best that they could despite their own conditioning and patterning. I share my experiences with compassion and love to inspire and offer hope to others. I no longer feel anger or ill intent from my past. Although I may not have liked some of the experiences I discuss and certainly don't want to live through them again, I can now see how they served me. As soon as I let regret or anger start to surface, I pause. For it was those very experiences that taught me resilience, empowerment, and compassion – that forced my Conqueress to awaken, that gave me passion and relentless tenacity, that brought me to this moment. I have never felt more aligned in mind, body, and soul. I have never felt such peace within, such purpose and clarity. I am thankful for those experiences. Only through them could I have been so fortunate to land exactly where I am.

Further, the more vulnerable we become, the more authentic we become, the more honest we can be about our reality, the more quickly we heal. This is the way of the Conqueress and aligning with our soul's purpose. Today I embrace the notion that life happens *for* me, never to me. All the heartache, emotional, and physical pain, all the unanswered questions, all the fear and doubt – it was all for me. Yes, at times the journey has been brutal. I wasn't always sure I could survive the agonizing torment and the paralyzing fear. Yet hope and determination kept me from drowning. The desire to unleash my Conqueress' radical self-love and become the role model my daughter deserved motivated me to keep moving forward. Shifting my perspective to a place of trust and gratitude allowed my path to become clearer and joy to fill my days. My experiences ignited a deep desire to be fully present in the moment and to appreciate all that I have, regardless of the chaos and negativity that may surround me. I honor and protect my inner peace. I dance, I laugh, and I am free because I restored the intimate connection of my mind, body, and soul. I learned to allow the Conqueress within to lead, guide, and empower me. And what I learned must be shared.

Introduction

In the pages of this book, I share some of my most vulnerable experiences in hopes that you may relate or gain perspective. They may also provide some insight into the hardship and pain of the human experience. And yet despite – or because of – such trials, we can experience transformative growth and find the Conqueress-like source of strength within. In addition to my personal testimonies, I also incorporate scientific, psychological, and spiritually based tools. I want to bridge some of the gaps between these three fundamental areas of the human journey.

Science Meets Spirituality

I have always had a strong sense of spirituality, but I haven't always been clear on or understand why I should do something. This may be a direct result of growing up in an authoritarian household and generation. Most of the people I speak to and work with relate to the concepts of being told what to do, of not being seen and or heard, and of never having the freedom to question authority. Now, as an adult, I want to know why. I want a reason. I want to understand.

Through mindfulness training, formal education, and some intuitive nudges, I found my way to a Sattva Yoga class. A Sanskrit term, *sattva* means balance, peace, and harmony. When combined with yoga, it promotes inner consciousness and personal awareness. These classes also incorporate *kriyas* (most commonly used in Kundalini), described as movements or energetic patterns involving one's "transcendental" self. To me they were awkward and odd, yet insanely powerful and transformative. When I surrendered to the movements, it was as though a powerful energy was moving through my body and being released. It felt nothing short of amazing, and later led me to India for a more in-depth experience.

At the same time, I had enrolled in some courses and training in neuropsychology. I became intrigued by the works of Dr. Peter Levine, Dr. Norman Doidge, and Bessel van der Kolk. I utilized several of their tools for myself and my clients with astonishing results. I was captivated by the capabilities of the "malleable brain." The idea of *neuroplasticity* – the ability of the physical brain to actually "rewire" itself and build new neural pathways – shed so much light on our capacity to heal from past trauma and create the life we desire.

As my understanding of neuropsychology grew, I noticed that certain practices with profound spiritual impacts – and scientific evidence of their effectiveness– utilize sound, repetition, vibration, movement, and imagery. These components have been shown to activate the vagus nerve (which controls the heart, lungs, and digestive track) and stimulate our frontal lobes. Further, they are derived from Polyvagal theory (poly-"many" + vagal "wandering"), a collection of evolutionary, neuroscientific and psychological claims pertaining to the role of the vagus nerve in emotion regulation, social connection and the fear response.

To understand how sound, repetition, vibration, movement, and imagery are experienced, think back to your childhood – or even more recently – and recall the experiences that brought you from distress to peace. It's highly likely that one or more of these five qualities were involved in the self-soothing process.

During my own childhood, when the farm chores were done and just after dinner, I would hear my grandmother's soft hum coming from the porch swing. I would climb up on the swing, trying not to disturb its gentle motion, and rock with her, listening to the gentle squeak as it hinged back and forth. Growing up Catholic, I remember finding comfort during the family rosary, allowing each bead to pass through my fingers in a repetitive rhythm, reciting the assigned prayer with a steady breath and a sense of comfort. When my daughter would get fussy as a baby, we knew to rock her and softly hum. When that didn't work, we would take her for a drive; the steady movement and humming of the engine would often lull her to sleep. And whether you perceive it as awkward or soothing, it is undeniable that the "Om" at the end of a yoga class brings about a beautiful sense of calm and wellbeing.

Each of these scenarios, whether intentionally or not, calms our central nervous system. Humming is a key technique for vibrating the vagus nerve; rocking elicits movement and repetition. That rocking sensation not only promotes memory and sleep maintenance,[1] but has been shown to activate the part of the brain that assists with regulating our thoughts and emotions.[2] Additionally, rocking provides a soothing sensation that belongs to our repertoire of adaptive behaviors in which the natural mechanism of sleep has been harnessed in the simplest manner since the times of our ancestral

---

[1] Aurore A. Perrault et al., "Whole-Night Continuous Rocking Entrains Spontaneous Neural Oscillations with Benefits for Sleep and Memory," *Current Biology* 29, no. 3 (February 2019): 402–11, https://doi.org/10.1016/j.cub.2018.12.028.

[2] Levine Peter, "Peter Levine PhD on Trauma: How the Body Releases Trauma and Restores Goodness," Digital Seminar (Live Webcast), *PESI*, May 1, 2018.

Conqueress.[3] And while the examples above didn't specifically use imagery, those quiet and peaceful environments opened up spaces for positive thoughts.

Again, these are the components that promote changes to our neural pathways, enhance the vagus nerve and our mind-body connection, and calm the nervous system. When the system is calm and we are fully connected, healing can – and will – occur. Such practices are an important part of the healing path I discovered that I will describe in this book.

Peeling the Onion

Having lived both extremes of the fear-to-bliss continuum, I am honored to share my experiences and what I learned with you. Making the shift from distress to peace can be a daunting task, which is why I break the tools and strategies I present into simple – but not always easy – steps. Throughout the book, I refer to these steps as "layers." Many therapeutic models refer to "peeling back the layers" (as you would with an onion). It's a metaphor for what takes place during the process of self-actualization, in which we learn to accept and embrace ourselves for the beings we were created to be. It's about taking the necessary time to peel back the layers of our conditioning to allow the Conqueress to emerge. It's also important to note that some layers may be thicker than others. And like the onion, peeling those layers may involve some tears. Whenever this happens, honor and acknowledge yourself while working through the four layers I describe in this book.

Each layer described below includes tools to help peel through the dense walls of self-preservation that you have used throughout your life. Those old patterns and defense mechanisms served a

[3] Laurence Bayer et al., "Rocking Synchronizes Brain Waves during a Short Nap," *Current Biology* 21, no. 12 (June 2011): R461–62, https://doi.org/10.1016/j.cub.2011.05.012.

purpose. They protected you, shielded you, and helped you avoid looking at things you weren't yet ready to fully see and experience. In childhood, you can be forgiven for falling under their spell, but as an adult, you are in control of your life and decisions. You no longer have to use these defenses. You are safe to have a voice. You are safe to make mistakes. You are safe to be authentic. It is safe to allow the Conqueress to be known. Know that everything happens at the right time. When we push or try to force solutions, the outcome doesn't always prove effective. Often, it can even be counterproductive. So sit back, breathe, and enjoy the journey.

Being denied an authentic expression of who we are makes us susceptible to self-doubt, people-pleasing, and codependent behaviors. It may cause us to question the future and live with fear. So much of this fear-based response has to do with the central nervous system. In the layers I describe, you will learn to calm your nervous system so that you can start responding to life from a place of trust and security rather than fear. Our overstimulated nervous systems have disconnected us from the mind-body-soul of our true nature. It is time to change and reprogram your thinking to serve your highest self – your Conqueress – using my four-step approach.

I have titled this approach F-E-A-T (FEAT). It corresponds to the following four layers: Feel, Explore, Acceptance, and Transform.

F- Feel: This first layer is crucial as you learn to develop and enhance your mind-body-soul connection by using the breath and meditation to become more mindful. These techniques will assist you in acknowledging your true self so that you can explore and embrace your feelings rather than push them away.

E- Explore: In this layer, you will begin to take a closer look at false or fear-based messages and identify the origination and source of these unwanted feelings. By understanding where they come from, you gain the power to begin to reprogram them.

A- Acceptance: This is a layer of both action and surrender. You will learn to recognize and accept what is within your control and what is not and, in that process, embrace "what is" and trust the outcome. You will also develop coping skills and strategies to navigate through anxious feelings.

T-Transform: Once you have cultivated self-awareness, you can start to reframe and transform unhealthy beliefs into healthy and beneficial ones, thus creating desirable new thought processes that align with the Conqueress within.

Within each of these layers, the Conqueress reveals her true and authentic self, the version within that seeks to be restored. Several tools are presented and described to help internalize each of the four layers. Additionally, you can access meditation recordings through *The Conqueress Guide to Overcoming Obstacles and Honoring Yourself* workbook on my website, DrMarcyB.com. The guide is an incredibly beneficial support and reference as you work through each of the layers. It will challenge you, support you, and keep you motivated as you progress on your Conqueress journey.

As you work through these layers, finding support will be critical. Here you learn to build community and connection and gain the realization that you are not alone, that we are all in this together. Having consistent support when you need it ties it all together and allows you to embark on the Conqueress path towards self-actualization.

How to Use this Book

If you resonate with this approach and feel called to live your life with purpose and alignment, I suggest reading this book in its entirety first to allow the concepts, tools, and experiences it conjures to marinate. Become mindful of how your highest self – the

Conqueress – responds and then start using the tools you feel most drawn to throughout your day. There are many tools, so don't be overwhelmed trying to incorporate them all at once. You'll know which ones you are drawn to and not, so use your intuition at first, then challenge yourself with deeper tools later if you desire.

Once you have finished the book and begun using some of the tools, find a support system or buddy. Accountability and connection are the keys to your healing. In my own recovery from divorce, codependency, addiction, low self-worth, and eating disorders, my healing occurred with connection. It's amazing how, when we struggle, the tendency of so many is to isolate, leading to beliefs of being abandoned and alone. We feel shame and guilt – also the story of a faulty belief system. I am here to tell you, such beliefs are not accurate.

All of our struggles are manifestations of how we learned to cope or survive in childhood as well as what was modeled for us. While these behaviors have been encoded in the brain, change is possible. We are not our struggles and we are not alone. As adults, we are able to develop new neural pathways, new coping skills, and new behaviors to show up for ourselves and to the world. For many years, I thought my struggles were unique. When I began to share them, the messages that came back to me were overwhelmingly of "Ditto," confirming that I was not alone. When we allow ourselves to become vulnerable, we not only heal but we also create space for others to open up and experience healing of their own. Once you have your support in place, go back through the layers as you feel guided. I suggest starting with one of the tools from Layer 1 first. If meditation is too new for you, start with just the breath work and allow the other tools to naturally unfold. From a psychological perspective, we are more likely to develop new habits when we start small. So often in healing, we want to over-achieve and do it all. At least I did. The result was an overstimulated nervous system and a sense of failure when I couldn't attain my lofty goals. Set realistic and attainable goals. Once a tool has become automatic like brushing your teeth, add a new one. As you do, all those seeds that were planted from each layer will continue to nourish and grow. Trust your intuition on how to proceed, remembering that this is a journey. Life will always have new challenges and lessons. The world is our playing field of non-stop practice.

As you travel through these layers, it is critical that you feel emotionally safe, experience an authentic expression of yourself, and are able to be fully and completely known and accepted for the beautiful being that you are. At the same time, it's not uncommon for family, friends, or colleagues that have known you to be a certain way to challenge or disapprove of your new actions and behaviors. This happens most frequently when we change our patterning or behavior toward those who have manipulated or controlled or even taken advantage of our goodness. When we begin to set healthy boundaries towards certain people that aren't used to us having a voice or just doing as told, we may be met with unfavorable words, actions, and emotions. And that's okay. Time heals and reveals. Those who truly want you to be your best self will come to accept and honor this shift. Ultimately, this book will allow you to embrace change and overcome barriers, to experience peace within regardless of the chaos that may swirl around you. As your journey unfolds through the four layers, may you continue to align with the wisdom, desires, and purpose of your inner Conqueress.

The Conqueress

She leads with a strong spine and a soft heart. The painted colors she wears on her face symbolize her imperfections; they animate her uniqueness rather than camouflaging her flaws. She expresses both her fierce love and righteous anger equally, without apology. Her eros and confidence are powerful attractors. A nurturing heart and compassion for others make her appeal even more formidable.

In the beginning of time, the Conqueress' survival depended on basic instincts: physically defending herself and foraging for food. And yet she still exalted her feminine qualities, embraced her femininity, loved with passion, and nobly mothered to ensure future generations. She trusted her intuition while seeking the grandiose power of the universe. Becoming self-sufficient and successfully navigating life's obstacles were – and still are – essential for her survival.

This fierce warrior energy still resides within all of us. It wants to be released, to be expressed, to be heard, to be known. And while our passionate warrior wisdom and instincts persists, we must recognize that their impulse to conquer and thrive looks much different in present-day experience. In short, we have evolved. In a rapidly advancing society full of technological changes, we have not kept up with the essential survival modes necessary to achieve wellness and self-actualization.

The Problem

As a society, we have not advanced our collective social-emotional well-being at the same rate that technology and science are requiring of us in order to evolve. Social media, online dating, online banking, ease of travel, and an abundance of information at our fingertips along with peer pressure, lack of privacy, and criticism in public spaces are the new normal. Break-ups, bullying, job promotions, the status of our children – all are on public display for everyone to see. Yet we often lose sight of the distortions of reality that come along with this. When it comes to social media, most people post only the positive scenarios – distorted images that everything is just fine when, in reality, the story is quite different. "Keeping up with the Jones" in this deceptive digital world has taken over our perceptions of what does and doesn't matter.

While we have demonstrated enormous gains in technology and science, we have lost touch with the intricate connection between the mind, body, and soul. In this modern quest for bigger, better, and more, we've become consumed – even obsessed – with trying to fulfill standards and achieve goals that others have defined for us. And when we "fail," we sink into depression and despair. Even when we succeed, the bliss is temporary, impossible to sustain because the standards others define us by rarely align with our soul's purpose. Until we re-establish the connection of mind, body, and soul, we cannot experience the bliss, peace, and purpose we were intended to fulfill. Until we can trust our intuition and allow the natural unfolding of life; chaos, anxiety, and depression will continue to govern our existence.

My cumulative experiences brought me to a breaking point, where I sought to reconnect my mind, body, and soul. As a living human being in a complex world, I value my spiritual connection for guidance in all that I do. My morning devotion and intention encapsulate my commitment to my purpose and reverence for my spiritual well-being. For me, it comes first each day. It shapes my reality and nourishes my soul.

A Holistic Perspective

As a health psychologist, my expertise is understanding the bio-psycho-social components of health and wellness. I look at things holistically and try to make sense of why we do the things we do and, more importantly, how to make them better. The mind is a profound mystery, and my background in educational psychology has helped me to understand brain functioning and behavior change and how to facilitate learning and transformation. When added to a deepened perspective into our common human challenges from significant and traumatic life experiences – both mine and others – I have come to understand that there are four specific areas in which we need to pivot and evolve so that we can continue our paths to wellness and self-actualization. They have to do with our biological, psychological, spiritual, and social well-being.

As I began to investigate and further my understanding of the mind, the topics of mindfulness and meditation continually surfaced. I advanced my knowledge by training in Mindfulness-Based Stress Reduction (MBSR) and began to establish my own practice. I later traveled to India where I began to bridge the gaps between my experience of science and spirituality. I found that many ancient practices of healing and transformation incorporate the use of sound, repetition, vibration, movement, and imagery. The impact of these components is also recognized in the field of neuropsychology and, more specifically, the phenomenon of *neuroplasticity*, suggesting that the intuitive nature of Eastern culture recognized their benefits long before the emerging research and scientific evidence of the West.

In simple terms, neuroplasticity refers to the brain's ability to rewire or reprogram itself. Why is this important?

1. The brain's neuronal patterns aren't fixed, which means that new pathways to the cortex can be created that lead to new processes and thinking patterns.[4,5,6]

2. It has long been believed that the adult brain is hardwired in a way and couldn't be changed. However, we now know that even the adult brain can be altered; it retains a degree of plasticity throughout its lifetime.[7,8]

3. Given this, we have the capacity to re-pattern and re-program ourselves to respond to life with healthier thoughts, emotions, and actions.[9,10,11]

---

[4] Jeffrey M. Schwartz and Sharon Begley, *The Mind and the Brain: Neuroplasticity and the Power of Mental Force* (New York: Regan Books/ Harper Collins Publishers, 2002).

[5] Norman Doidge, *The Brain That Changes Itself: Stories of Personal Triumph from the Frontiers of Brain Science* (Victoria, Australia: Scribe Publications, 2010).

[6] Eric Jensen, *Enriching the Brain: How to Maximize Every Learner's Potential* (New Jersey: John Wiley & Sons, 2009).

[7] Schwartz and Begley, *The Mind and the Brain.*

[8] Jensen, *Enriching the Brain.*

[9] Natascha Schaefer et al., "The Malleable Brain: Plasticity of Neural Circuits and Behavior - a Review from Students to Students," *Journal of Neurochemistry* 142, no. 6 (August 8, 2017): 790–811, https://doi.org/10.1111/jnc.14107.

[10] Doidge, *The Brain That Changes Itself.*

[11] Doidge, *The Brain That Changes Itself.*

As we have evolved as a species, our basic needs are much more easily met. This permits us to move up Maslow's hierarchy of needs and work toward the self-actualization we all desire. What we have failed to recognize, though, are the bio-psycho-social shifts required to get there. We are born with survival instincts, but skills such as boundary setting, healthy coping, and stress management must be taught and learned. Our primitive counterparts relied primarily on the lower brain for survival. Today, we need to utilize our executive functioning skills in the cerebral cortex. We find our best thinking when we activate the frontal lobes of the brain. This is where we organize our thoughts, apply logic and reason, and plan and monitor our actions and behaviors. When we default to the lower brain, we activate our central nervous system which sends a message to our brain that we are in crisis – even when we aren't. This is the origin of "fight, flight, or freeze." Rewiring the brain and calming the nervous system requires deliberate, intentional, and repetitive training. When the central nervous system is calm, our frontal lobes are stimulated, and we begin to experience the best version of ourselves.

Unfortunately, the focus on status, achievement, and monetary advances leaves little room for true well-being. Fortunately, the more time we take to calm our central nervous system and gain the skills and tools needed to advance toward self-actualization, the more likely we will be able to fulfill our ambitions, whatever they may be. The more connected we become to our intuition, the easier it will be to discern where true happiness and success reside.

Furthermore, there is an unspoken notion that one cannot be both scientific and spiritual. Academics often mock or critique the idea of spirituality because it lacks the validity of scientific data. They perceive any investigation into the nature of spirituality as unethical or unscientific. It is simply too intangible or unintellectual. On the opposite side of the spectrum, many spiritual gurus discount and/ or disregard the findings of science and psychological research as unnecessary and missing the point. They adhere to the belief systems of their religious or spiritual advisors and traditions.

The reality is that spirituality and religion are central to the lives of the majority of people. In fact, most adults express a belief in a God[12] and identify religion as one of the most influential factors in their lives (although specific beliefs around such mysteries as death and miracles will vary). Yet, while spirituality is commonly regarded as an integral component of the human experience, it hasn't received adequate attention within medical and therapeutic settings. Some suggest this may be the result of a lack of basic understanding, doubt regarding its relevance and how to address it, or difficulty in explaining how spirituality may be of benefit to patients.[13]

Spirituality, though a relatively broad concept, has recently been formulated into a conceptual framework and approach helping to elevate the term for proper acknowledgement and status as a researchable topic. Having such a framework allows it to be inclusive, accessible, relevant, and applicable to more practitioners within the medical and health professions.[14] Research studies have shown that incorporating spiritual interventions into medicine has benefitted physical and emotional health and is an alternative desired by patients.[15],[16] These results are making it easier to utilize spirituality in therapeutic settings. As spiritual beliefs are taken more seriously,

---

[12] Richard Swinburne, *The Existence of God* (Oxford, England: Oxford University Press on Demand, 2004).

[13] Dana E. King and Bruce Bushwick, "Beliefs and Attitudes of Hospital Inpatients about Faith Healing and Prayer," *Journal of Family Practice* 39, no. 4 (October 1994): 349–52.

[14] Philip J. Siddall, Melanie Lovell, and Rod MacLeod, "Spirituality: What Is Its Role in Pain Medicine?," *Pain Medicine* 16, no. 1 (January 2015): 51–60, https://doi.org/10.1111/pme.12511.

[15] Joshua A. Williams et al., "Attention to Inpatients' Religious and Spiritual Concerns: Predictors and Association with Patient Satisfaction," *Journal of General Internal Medicine* 26, no. 11 (July 1, 2011): 1265–71, https://doi.org/10.1007/s11606-011-1781-y.

[16] Jeffrey E. Barnett, "Are Religion and Spirituality of Relevance in Psychotherapy?," *Spirituality in Clinical Practice* 3, no. 1 (2016): 5–9, https://doi.org/10.1037/scp0000093.

it becomes a source of strength and hope while validating influence on one's life and daily experiences.

Scientific Insights

Science is science; data is data. Research studies have merit. Having both a Doctorate and a Master's degree, I've experienced education, science, and research as being of great value. I constantly promote and encourage learning and advancing our studies and knowledge. I strive to be a life-long learner and hope the same for my daughter.

Fortunately, today's generation is encouraged to question and challenge both authority and information. They demand to know why, how, and what. They want to know their options, the repercussions, and the benefits. While this can be exhausting for a parent, keep encouraging your kids – or any child – to ask questions, seek truth, and expand their knowledge. It's okay to allow Alexa or Google or Siri to field some of those non-stop questions for you!

However, always be mindful of where your information comes from as well as the tendency to overgeneralize. Obviously not everything on the internet is true. Use reliable sources. Trust professionals for big decisions. I'm sure I'm not the only one who has read diagnostic criteria on the web and exaggerated symptoms of a mosquito bite or convinced myself that I had a terminal disease. It has become a common laughing point among those in my profession about how easy it is to read our fears into vague diagnostic criteria and then want to self-diagnose on a tough day. Fortunately, I've discovered my voice of reason and trusted my intuition to help me identify such irrational thoughts. Regardless of your education and knowledge, your intuition is the key to decision making and a profound knowing. More than any book, I have found that intuition gives us access to information we may not otherwise know, and everyone deserves to free it in themselves.

In sum, we are fortunate to have access to science, literature, and research to provide us with the answers to many of our questions. In my doctoral research, I realized how important research is for bridging the gaps between what is known and what we need to understand. Each new piece of data helps us to keep advancing and thriving. While science can provide us with knowledge and information, our spiritual intuition helps guide the decisions we make from that information. As such, it is possible – even necessary – to have both a strong spiritual guidance system and a deep respect for scientific data. By expanding the possibilities that mind, body, and soul are equally relevant, the personal journey to expansion, healing, and wholeness can occur. I have heard the concept compared to a three-legged stool. Like the legs of the stool, each part – the mind, body, and soul – are equally essential in part and purpose. If one part is lacking, we lose our balance and can no longer serve with purpose. And in today's often ego-centric and unpredictable world, we need all the balance we can get.

The Four Shifts

Physical Shift

The Conqueress was brave. She was fierce in all that she did. She conquered with a zealous passion and fought with an untamed spirit.

*   *   *

The bravery and fierceness of our ancestral Conqueress allowed her to escape from tigers, fend for food and shelter, and overcome mountains. While we are now "advanced humans" with great purpose, that Conqueress energy persists within and the definition of brave and fierce has evolved. The Conqueress of the modern world shows her fierceness and bravery in how she sets boundaries, stands up for herself, and pursues her dreams. From a biological or physical perspective, let's consider how this ages-old evolution aligns with the modern Conqueress.

The notion of "survival of the fittest" has changed drastically between then and now. Survival of the ancestral Conqueress meant meeting one's basic needs: food, safety, and shelter for survival. Our "lower brain," often associated with the "fight, flight, or freeze" response, was the ancestral Conqueress's essential tool for survival. Today, those basic needs are met more easily, leaving time to scale different mountains – more specifically, self-actualization. To get there, we must retrain ourselves to use the higher-level thinking skills found in the brain's frontal lobes.

Fortunately, we now know it is possible to change or "rewire" the brain. We understand that the brain is malleable (neuroplasticity), and that by adjusting and modifying our thought processes and behaviors, we are literally changing the brain itself. While this takes conscious and deliberate effort, the results and outcomes are worth the effort. Further, the tools included in this book contain the necessary elements to initiate and sustain these changes. While the *science* of neuroplasticity is robust, it is also cumbersome to wade through. The *practice* of it, however, is much easier.

When you came into the world, you were of pure love, pure peace, and complete worthiness. You still are. As adults, we don't always remember this. Life experiences and the patterns developed during our lifetime may have led us to have negative self-talk, low self-esteem, and unhealthy habits. That universal truth then becomes distorted and the light within is dimmed.

Our patterns of behavior are like railroad tracks in the brain. The tracks are the path we take to process events, act and behave. They are the stories we tell about ourselves. The more we tell the same story, the more likely we take the same track or path. For example, if the tracks you have imprinted in your brain tell you to stay small or not to speak up because you feel unworthy or that your opinion doesn't matter, this becomes a conditioned pattern. Each time such an opportunity arises, your automatic (and inaccurate) response will be a "no" because you feel that you don't deserve it. These are the changes that need to be fixed. This is where the neural pathways of the brain need to be re-patterned. You are worthy and you always have been.

While these tracks will always remain, the more you create new tracks – new paths – to process the same information, the more power and control you gain. We can create new pathways to arrive at the same destination or to head in an entirely different direction.

Creating these new tracks offers new opportunities and opens your world to the abundance of experiences that are available to you. Further, the more conscious we become of our thoughts, the more likely we'll know the best route to take.

This book describes a simplified process that will expand your knowledge and provide you with tools to heal your mind, body, and soul. This healing is a restoration from disease, imbalance, trauma, and other damage you've experienced throughout your lifetime. It involves the re-unification of the balance between mind, body, and soul. Healing means becoming vulnerable, unapologetic about being fully known, forgiving ourselves and others, setting healthy parameters around the actions of ourselves and others, and coming into alignment with the core of who we are. With this healing, you can honor yourself and find your passion and purpose. Your life flows with ease and grace. You unleash your Conqueress.

Neural Re-Patterning

To begin, you will notice an emphasis on the use of sound, vibration, repetition, movement, and imagery throughout the book. These components are crucial to balancing an over-stimulated and noisy brain. They help restore homeostasis – the stability and balance of your body's systems.

This process of changing the brain starts with *neurostimulation:* regulating and modulating your thoughts and behaviors.[17] Also important when harnessing the power of the brain is physical health. Neurons that are free of infection, toxins, and chemicals and frequently replenished with adequate nutrition are better equipped to connect, communicate, and rebuild. Once homeostasis and health are achieved, the brain will be ready to create new pathways and eliminate unhealthy patterns.

In the second stage, called *neuromodulation*, the focus is on

---

[17] Doidge, *The Brain That Changes Itself.*

calming the autonomic nervous system and turning off the fight, flight, or freeze response.[18] This will send a message of calmness to the brain. One of the most effective ways to do this is by activating the vagus nerve. The vagus is the most important nerve of the parasympathetic nervous system; it is involved in the healing response and generating feelings of calmness and wellbeing. The translation of *vagus* is "wanderer," which aptly represents its widespread influence over the cortex, brainstem, hypothalamus, and the body.[19] The vagus nerve is becoming more frequently researched and has been referred to as the "mind-body superhighway."

The back part of the vagus nerve, called the dorsal vagus, correlates with the lower, primitive brain ("fight, flight, or freeze"), while the ventral vagus in the front activates our frontal lobes. This stimulation in the frontal lobes allows the mind and body to be in the flow state. That's why it's important to improve *vagal tone*, also referred to as *vagus nerve stimulation*. The purpose of improving vagal tone is to help the ventral vagal complex work more efficiently. When it does, it becomes easier to bring about homeostasis with the body and stimulation to the frontal lobes.

Strategies that have been shown to improve vagal tone include meditation, deep breathing, gargling, singing, and chanting.[20],[21],[22] Positive social connections that include laughter, sharing,

---

[18] Doidge, *The Brain That Changes Itself.*

[19] Kesava Mandalaneni and Appaji Rayi, *Vagus Nerve Stimulator* (Florida: StatPearls Publishing, 2021).

[20] Venugopal R. Damerla et al., "Novice Meditators of an Easily Learnable Audible Mantram Sound Self-Induce an Increase in Vagal Tone during Short-Term Practice: A Preliminary Study," *Integrative Medicine: A Clinician's Journal* 17, no. 5 (October 1, 2018): 20–28.

[21] James D'Angelo, *The Healing Power of the Human Voice: Mantras, Chants, and Seed Sounds for Health and Harmony* (Vermont: Inner Traditions/Bear & Co, 2005).

[22] Eva Detko, *Mind-Body and the Vagus Nerve Connection Transcripts [Transcripts from Seven Day Training from Various Professionals Regarding the Vagus Nerve]*, 2020, Ebook.

authenticity, and nonjudgmental relationships also help re-establish and strengthen our mind-body connection. Exercise and movement, specifically interval training and weightlifting as well as walking and rocking motions, are also correlated with improved vagal tone. Cold exposure therapy is a relatively new concept that is shown to assist with the mind-body connection. Each of these tools allow us to become more aware of our thoughts and emotions. Over time, balance is restored between the excitation and inhibition in our neural networks and we can begin to quiet the mental chatter.

In the third stage, *neurorelaxation*, we flourish in a state of tranquility while our neurons continue to regenerate.[23] We begin to understand, change ourselves, and reconnect the mind, body, and soul when the ventral vagus is activated, leading to a calm central nervous system; behavior change and emotional healing cannot occur in any other state because only then can we take more conscious control of our thoughts and feelings. We recalibrate our internal rhythms to the parasympathetic "rest and relax" response instead of being in constant overdrive and overstimulation from the lower brain's "fight, flight or freeze."

Neurodifferentation represents the fourth stage of reprogramming our malleable brains.[24] As children, the lack of appropriate co-regulation, attention, and modeling of healthy behaviors may have resulted in underdeveloped skills, faulty belief systems, and undesirable habits. Co-regulation is the positive and responsive interactions that provide the support, coaching, and modeling children need to "understand, express, and modulate their thoughts, feelings, and behaviors."[25] The goal of co-regulating is to promote

---

[23] Doidge, *The Brain That Changes Itself.*

[24] Doidge, *The Brain That Changes Itself.*

[25] Desiree W. Murray et al., "Self-Regulation and Toxic Stress: Foundations for Understanding Self-Regulation from an Applied Developmental Perspective (OPRE Report #2015-21)" (Washington, DC: Office of Planning, Research and Evaluation, Administration for Children and Families, US Department of Health and Human Services, 2015).

the development of self-regulation, or the "conscious control of thoughts, feelings, and behaviors."[26] Without this guidance as a child, it is difficult to know what to do with feelings, emotions, and thoughts as they arise. As a result, unhealthy coping mechanisms may be developed.

Additionally, impulsive behavioral patterns with roots in the lower brain's fight, flight, or freeze response may have also given rise to patterns of unhealthy thoughts and emotions. Despite such pathways being ingrained, when we establish a calm nervous system, we are able to use logic to create new pathways and responses and begin to create the life we desire and were born to live.

The Brain Supports You

The tools and strategies of the Conqueress align with the stages of neuroplastic change. The goal is to rewire the brain's current thought and behavior patterns by altering the connections and pathways between neurons. For example, the tools presented in the first layer of reprogramming – Feel – allow the body to return to homeostasis by activating the parasympathetic nervous system, which is required for neurostimulation, neuromodulation, neurorelaxation, and neurodifferentiation, described above. Such practices as meditation and breathwork are key in preparing the brain to change and evolve by allowing the overstimulated brain to rest so it can resume its purpose of making distinctions between desirable and undesirable outcomes. Therefore, when the first layer is situated, one is ready to approach the next three layers of Explore, Acceptance, and Transformation.

The Explore layer will help you identify where false past beliefs, messages, or habits may have originated. Such understanding leads

---

[26] Megan M. McClelland and Shauna L. Tominey, "The Development of Self-Regulation and Executive Function in Young Children," *Zero to Three* 35, no. 2 (2014): 2–8.

to compassion for yourself, your situation, and the lives of those around you. Again, this emotional healing is only possible when we are calm and the parasympathetic nervous system has been activated. The Explore layer goes deeper to establish a balance between trusting our intuition and surrendering our egos, which enables Acceptance of our empowered Conqueress life. Finally, the Transform layer provides the opportunity to truly define what we want and how we want to show up in life. It is here, in the final layer, that we have finally evolved into our empowered, Conqueress self.

Support is crucial to the healing and recovery process. Support systems promote a sense of empowerment as well as connection through interpersonal relationships and social inclusion. Once "transformed," we intuitively seek them out to establish a sense of safety that allows us to thrive. It's about anchoring the positive identity you have cultivated – necessary for sustaining the healing and recovery from patterns that haven't served you. The prefrontal cortex needs positive and supportive social connections to reprogram at full capacity.

Psychological Shift

$\mathcal{S}$he danced and sang in her tribal circle. She screamed and released her rage. She laughed with unrestrained excitement. She prayed and trusted her spiritual guidance. Her priority was ensuring that her psychological and safety needs were met.

*   *   *

In the Western world, we are fortunate to have fewer concerns about having enough food, water, and shelter. We generally feel physically safe and secure. Because of that, we are more in touch with our innate desire to reach our highest level of self-actualization. We strive for belongingness and love. We seek to improve our esteem with prestige and feelings of accomplishment. With the rapid advancement of technology and overall quality of life, the psychological evolution has been one of the most substantial of our time. Yet we seem to pay little respect nor reverence to our rudimentary needs of emotional safety and security.

In large part, it's because we are not equipped to handle the psychological challenges of a status-driven, highly scrutinized, judgmental, and ego-driven society. Instead, we avoid or escape from the intense emotions by numbing out with medications, food, alcohol, cigarettes, or other unhealthy habits. Rates of anxiety, depression, addiction, and mood disorders, along with prescriptions for antidepressants, continue to climb.

These behaviors are fear-based and stem from a lower-brain response. When we become stuck at that level of functioning, we make impulsive, illogical decisions that often lead to unhealthy habits and addictions and create self-perpetuating neuropathways. While the function of this part of the brain is to protect us, it is not sophisticated enough to understand the complex needs of our modern Conqueress.

What if, for just a moment, you stopped and took a deep breath to calm the nervous system? What if you allowed yourself to feel and embrace sensations as they arise, whether "good" or "bad"? What if you allowed yourself to look at the harder ones with curiosity instead of always pushing them away? What if you began to recognize that the emotions will persist until you acknowledge them? What if your feelings are a message, a signal from the body, trying to communicate that something isn't right? Most of the time, when something "isn't right," it's because we are responding to life from a place of fear and false, outdated beliefs.

Much of this faulty wiring stems from the unhealthy conditioning and patterning that we received as children. The experiences we had and the modeling we observed ultimately set the tone for how we see ourselves and learned to function or survive in the world. For many, this realization may surface intense anger and resentment toward the adults and guardians in our lives. I remember feeling this resentment during times in my life that I perceived as hard or unfair. I wanted to blame all my problems on my parenting or the lack of it.

In truth, as we have evolved and our basic needs are more easily met, our psychological needs become more relevant. The generations before us did what they could with what they were given. They were never taught the skills or given certain tools to pass to the next generation. From a place of deep reflection and empathy,

I have compassion for them. Nevertheless, those influences, and the desire to better the next generation, have brought us to where we are today. We have evolved so rapidly that while the priority was once to hunt and gather and protect our offspring, we now prioritize healthy relationships, career goals, beauty and appearance, and physical health and wellness. Only recently have we started to discuss how to set healthy boundaries, handle peer pressure, and create balance in our life. And yet the skills we need to cultivate our psychological wellbeing need to be learned and taught. At the same time, technical advancements as mobile phones, the internet, and social media have made it increasingly more difficult to catch up with our psychological needs.

As we address the psychological shifts we need to make, we can thrive as a Conqueress in today's society. We will experience a peaceful shift to greater acceptance of "what is" while empowering ourselves to initiate change rather than fester in resentment and anger. It's important to note that while we develop compassion and understanding around our childhood experiences, this doesn't mean that those years were healthy or acceptable nor that we are doomed to stay stuck in the same patterns. In this phase, take time to validate your emotions and yield to the process. By choosing to discover your own power, you will pass those skills and tools onto the next generation and keep the cycle of evolution moving forward.

Social Shift

$\mathcal{S}$he came from a tribe, a family that valued unity, loyalty, and trust. The Conqueress acted in the best interest of her tribe, knowing her survival depended on it. She was supported and nurtured in a manner designed for survival. While attention and affection may not always have been obvious, it was not as essential as her basic needs being met. When met, she was satisfied. Through the evolution of time, those basic social needs have stayed the same. While the culture has shifted, the fierceness of the Conqueress persists.

*　　*　　*

In our present-day world, competition, judgment, and comparisons have become the norm. Community and belonging lost its importance. Even within families, competitiveness and the lack of love, attention, and affection can create wounds and scars that go unnoticed and may never heal. Most families are full of bandage solutions that push pain into the shadows where they go unseen. The conflict of intra-family disconnection resonates deeply in the Conqueress who innately desires a sense of family and unity. When it's not in her best interest to maintain those connections and the need for boundaries is clear, she stays true to her Conqueress self. Even as her heart breaks in a million pieces seeing the hurt and anger of loved ones, fierce self-love always comes first as she sets boundaries and honors herself.

Today, most societies and families have their basic needs intact, making the desire for affection, attention, self-esteem, and identity next in line to move toward self-actualization. While it's healthy and normal to feel frustrated or angry if you were deprived of those experiences while growing up, it is equally healthy and *more* productive to re-train yourself and achieve these qualities. In doing so, you'll discover self-compassion and a sense of pride for taking such an initiative which will please the Conqueress within. Many women get stuck in anger or denial and never get to experience the fierce power of being a Conqueress. By limiting themselves and staying stagnant, they are also less able to teach and model healthy coping skills and strategies for future generations.

The rewards are deeply gratifying for those who have learned to create new neural pathways while teaching ourselves to navigate life with ease and grace. When you have lived both sides, when you have experienced the pain and then the triumph, you are motivated to keep growing and you are filled with gratitude for that gift.

Modern Life

Our social lives are far from private, while our day-to-day tasks require critical thinking. Whereas our ancestors' survival depended on lower-brain functioning, we no longer rely on it and yet we often overstimulate the area by being in an ongoing state of anxiety and stress. This persistent fear is driven by perceived threats. We keep playing out scenarios to "stay ahead," analyzing different options and various outcomes, always choosing bigger, better, and more; none of which actually threaten our lives. But our mind doesn't know the difference between real and imagined. So, as we continue to imagine these negative scenarios, our brains process and encode them as if we are having the experience. The perceived pressure continually activates the fight, flight, or freeze response, placing us in a constant state of stress, unable to heal or change.

Personally, I have found this phenomenon to be especially true regarding socialization and relationships. While the Conqueress of the past was limited in exposure to her immediate family and circle of friends, today we face the often daunting and exhausting tasks of online dating and social media. To be clear, I don't think any of the new-found digital world is negative. It's just different. We are fortunate to have so many options and opportunities. Technology can be healthy as long as we align with the platform from our empowered self.

Unfortunately, what I often see happening in social media is pressure or desire to meet certain standards, gain the approval of others, and be selected. This "less than" mentality doesn't align with the Conqueress standard of empowerment – the Conqueress who knows who she is and does not conform. She uses the options and opportunities to find companionship that aligns with her core values. When a relationship doesn't work out, she doesn't take it personally. She accepts that two people can both be good people but not necessarily a great match. She well-wishes others and isn't spiteful. The Conqueress is compassionate and accepting. She is open to her own evolution and isn't afraid to make mistakes. In so doing, she stands her ground and maintains fierce integrity. Her boundaries do not waiver and she does not conform to gain the approval or attention of others. It's this confidence that declares her as both alluring and brave.

With healthy coping skills intact, the Conqueress chooses social connections that support an authentic expression of who she is as her highest self. In a healthy union or partnership, she is honest about who she is and what she stands for and demands the same rigorous honesty in a partner. Therefore, they promote and raise each other up. There is no judgement. There is no shame. There is only love and acceptance.

Spiritual Shift

The Conqueress relies on her intuition and spends a significant amount of time and devotion in spiritual connection. She knows bliss. She trusts that life is unfolding exactly as it is meant to. She avoids comparisons, knowing that what aligns with her soul and brings her purpose can vary greatly from that of others. She carries peace regardless of the chaos that may swirl around her.

*   *   *

As humans evolved, a rift developed where we stopped trusting ourselves, choosing instead to seek the advice and influence of others rather than rely on our own spiritual guidance system. The Conqueress places her trust in something greater than herself, knowing that control is an illusion. She is aware that trying to manipulate and manage life is a daunting and unproductive task. The Conqueress takes action and leaves the outcome to something more powerful, more loving, more knowing that she can comprehend. She trusts with a spirit of gratitude.

Even as they look to others for advice, most people today spend much of their time and energy trying to control and manipulate, thinking that if they act or manage in a certain way, they will obtain a desired outcome. Nothing could be further from the truth. Deep within, our Conqueress is aware of disconnection and desires instead to re-establish the connection between mind-body-soul, confident in the knowledge that her spiritual, intuitive self knows what is best and desires above all to keep her safe and protected.

The terms *spirit* and *soul* are often used interchangeably. One's spirit has been described as the nonphysical part of a person – the seat of emotions and character. Similarly, the soul is labeled as the immaterial part of one's being. But to me, there is a difference.

The soul exists within us. It is where the Conqueress resides. It is where we gather wisdom from the mind, the body, and whatever spiritual or higher guidance you choose to trust. The soul is the core of who you are. The spirit is an external and invisible source of love and guidance that gives your soul strength, purpose, and knowing. The gifts of spirit can come in many forms such as one's "God," or the Universe, or a Higher Power. Our spiritual connection is what brings us nearer to the God of our understanding.

I have heard the testimonials of others, such as trusting a nudge to take a different route home from work and later finding out there was a fatal accident on the typical route, or "getting a message" of where to look to find a sentimental missing item. There are also the examples of visual reminders that appear exactly when we need to see them. Hummingbirds, butterflies, and rainbows, for example, often serve as reminders of a spiritual connection to our intuition and a greater wisdom. Other hints include a chance encounter with just the right person, a thought or conviction that keeps growing, a verse or quote which comes to mind, something said in conversation which stays with you, or an opportunity which suddenly opens up or won't go away no matter what you or anyone else does to push it back or ignore it.

Although such experiences vary from person to person as does their meaning, they usually offer hope and restore faith in the greater good. That intuitive voice of reason resides within each of us. Our spiritual wellbeing is essential to helping us balance the mind, body, and soul on our three-legged stool.

My most profound experiences of spiritual knowledge served as a reminder to trust myself – to *always* trust myself. That alone is very empowering. Trusting myself means accepting that my intuition will guide me toward my next right step. It also means knowing that sometimes I will need to listen to the advice of others, ask for help, or admit my mistakes. Listening to my intuition and the guidance within has kept me on my path in times of uncertainty and despair.

During my daily meditation and prayer, I establish the connection between my mind, body, and soul. Each day, I attempt to follow the instinct that arises from this trinity. When I fully listen, my day flows with ease and clarity. The days when I am not as interconnected, I find myself trying to control or manipulate, often with frustration and anxiety. If I am paying attention, this tension will remind me of the power of my spiritual self.

A profound experience in my twenties made it abundantly clear why I should trust the voice of my intuitive reason, even when I don't understand why. Although it was well over twenty years ago, the energy and feelings still surface when I think about it. It was late afternoon and I decided to go for a jog in the neighborhood near the apartment that my college roommates and I shared. About a mile or so into the jog, I felt a sense of fear, that something wasn't right. There was nothing abnormal about the situation and going for a jog was part of my routine. Yet my intuitive instincts were strong, urging me to listen and obey *now*. I eventually found myself so full of trepidation that I had sped up my pace and, rather than staying on the running path, was literally running in the middle of the road!

Moments later, a perpetrator struck me from the side and pushed me to the ground. I screamed like I have never screamed before. I don't think I even stopped to take a breath for what seemed like an eternity. Thankfully, my fight, flight, or freeze response was in high gear. I kicked him in the groin and pushed and kicked and punched until I got myself up off the ground, at which point he fled. His face, his energy, his aura – I can still see them after all these years.

The police were called and eventually I had to identify him in some mug shots and line-ups that were later used to investigate incidents of three other college females who had been assaulted. I am grateful that I had that spiritual connection, the intuitive wisdom, and the willingness to listen. Had I not listened to that internal cue or trusted myself to do what felt right and safe – even though it wasn't logical – I may have found myself in a traumatic situation that could have damaged my wellbeing.

That powerful and protective force resides within us all.

Stop.
Take a breath.
Listen.
Do you hear her?
She is ready.
Now is the time.

The Value of Support

Truth. Companionship. Reverence.

The Conqueress, with her fierce focus, discipline, and finesse, never hesitated to be fully open to life. She was who she was, unapologetically. Those around her supported and embraced this creative expression of her true self. There were no comparisons; there were no judgments. She was allowed to be authentic in her actions and desires. Just as she was supported, she reciprocated with the same reverence and respect.

*   *   *

As you work through the four layers, your empowered Conqueress will be unveiled. You will feel her, embrace her, and love her. At the same time, it is vitally important that your support system do the same. In choosing who is part of that support system, be wise. A healthy support system will allow you to be completely authentic without judgment or shame. It will help you to feel emotionally safe, to have a voice, and to be fully heard and accepted. Connect with others who challenge you to step out of your comfort zone and who you can "agree to disagree" with. These support systems will not only nourish your soul as you travel through your transformations but help you build life and coping skills – skills that weren't taught to us as children. Since we aren't born with this knowledge, our learning previously depended on what our families modeled, which became the baseline for normal. It was all we knew, but far from healthy or effective.

Many of my friends and acquaintances have shared similar experiences of growing up in households where children were taught to be "seen and not heard." Questioning authority was unforgivable; you were to do as you were told, without logic or reason. Over time, we stop believing that our feelings or opinions matter, that we have a voice, that we deserve to be trusted and respected. These wounds run deep; the scarring is on the inside, not visible to others. These are the wounds and scars that require the most attention, love, and healing. Until we trust ourselves and are able to both hold our own space and allow others to hold space for us in a safe, loving, and supportive setting, our healing journey will not be as easy.

Remember that nothing has to be permanent. If your support system or one of its members isn't working out, it's okay to make a change. I truly believe that each person who has come into my life, no matter how long they stayed, served a purpose. Perhaps there was a message I needed to hear or one I needed to share. Maybe it was to give or receive love or to discover what I will and won't stand for. We grow, we love, and we evolve. This happens often in a recovery and healing process. As we grow, our needs change. It may be uncomfortable and unfamiliar, but think of each shift, each change in your life, as an experiment. So often we go through life with all-or-nothing, black-or-white thinking. The truth is, we spend most of our lives in grey, a beautifully complex blend of both black and white.

Permit Authenticity

How the support comes and where the support comes will be unique to each person. For some, it may include psychotherapy or some form of counseling. For others, it may include having an accountability partner or social network. I suggest using a hybrid of both individual counseling and support groups. For me, seeing a therapist was extremely powerful. I don't think I would have gained my clarity and resolve as effectively or even at all without it. Again, this is your journey. Your journey is yours and only yours to unfold. Accept that your journey may take you along different paths. Stay open.

Support groups, both formal and informal, can be a great complement to individualized therapy, and just as empowering and insightful. First, they provide hope and the awareness that you aren't alone; there are many, many others who've had similar experiences. In support groups, it's important to both give and receive, to both support and be of service. Some situations of those in the group may seem easier or more intense than yours. But to those individuals, it was traumatic and that's what matters. Again, I point this out because we often assume traumas are intense catastrophes such as domestic or family violence, dating violence, community violence (shooting, mugging, burglary, assault, bullying), sexual or physical abuse, natural disaster such as a hurricane, flood, fire or earthquake, or a serious car accident. It is not always so obvious. Trauma is specific to its impact on an individual and their interpretation of the experience. It can be emotional *or* physical.

As a society, we are starting to recognize the validity of each individual's unique interpretation of an event, so it's important to honor yourself in this way as well. Unfortunately, many of the people I have interacted with feel shame or guilt for responding the way they do, thinking others have it worse or that "My life isn't so bad." While this *may* be true, it is not a good reason to negate your own feelings. This also means refraining from comparing yourself or your situation to that of another. The only valid comparison is of ourselves from one day to the next. Be true to yourself. By honoring your experience and working through the layers, you can recover, you can overcome, and you can conquer.

From both personal and professional experience, I can tell you that the power of social support is substantial. With the advances and options now available through technology, the possibilities are many. One word of caution, though: don't overwhelm yourself. Overextending and losing integrity with your social commitments can be stressful and counterproductive.

I recall being a member of three support groups. Additionally, I had an accountability buddy who I spoke with every day and I was supporting two mentees. That commitment, combined with all my other responsibilities, roles, and obligations, was just too much. While I enjoyed and adored the people in these groups, keeping up with and responding to them all took a lot of energy. And yet I was reluctant to give them up because I did find value in both giving and receiving support.

Instead, I decided to set a boundary for myself. I let go of the expectation that I needed to listen and respond to every message. Rather, I would comment and touch base *as needed*. In that way, I still had a support system in times of distress without the obligational anxiety.

Many people struggle with isolation and not having enough support. They isolate themselves during times when support is most needed. Although reaching out can feel unfamiliar and generate feelings of vulnerability, that simple action can yield astonishing results. The power of support and connection is priceless. Find the right balance between isolation and overload.

The right support group should provide a protective barrier while on your path to healing and recovery. It is also crucial to be aware if others' stories, advice, or support is triggering you in some way or isn't helpful. If you start to feel stressed, take some time to understand what isn't working for you. Your personal mission is to align with and honor your own belief system, and you may be working through the previous layer or some hard issues. If this is the case, it may feel uncomfortable or unfamiliar. That's okay. Sit with it. Get curious about the emotion coming up for you.

A critical component of claiming your authenticity in a support system is allowing yourself to be fully known. True healing occurs when we become brutally honest about our thoughts, feelings, and actions. This honesty builds integrity and allows us to begin to trust ourselves. It is the key to behavior change and healing. True healing occurs when we can acknowledge and accept our own short-comings and share those feelings with trusted others who support your journey. This is why support groups are so beneficial. It may be the first time in your life that you connect with others who just "get it," who accept you for who you are. They can often relate to your experience and provide a level of support and love that seems almost unfathomable coming from a stranger. It is from these shared experiences and suffering that we discover a profound sense of belonging and compassion for others.

Give and Receive

You are wise and strong. But that doesn't always mean having to do everything yourself or pushing through tough times alone. We weren't designed to navigate this world in isolation. We are social beings; we rely on community. There is nothing wrong with asking others for help. In fact, discovering your inner Conqueress can sometimes only be done with the help of others. It is also wise and strong to identify and honor your vulnerabilities. That doesn't mean being weak in times of fear but loving yourself through the fear and knowing when to reach out for support.

In a traditional therapeutic setting, the roles of the therapist and patient are clearly established. In 12-Step settings (a program that originated in Alcoholics Anonymous), a sponsor-member relationship is established where the sponsor mentors the "spon-see" by offering advice and support. In more informal social support groups settings, whether in person or online, these roles are reciprocated. When serving in the role of the listener or giver, do just that. Listen. Listen with your ears and your heart. Allow the other to be heard and speak their truth. Advice should not be offered without solicitation. Rather, validate and affirm what was said. Share your vulnerable experiences and stories of resilience, wisdom, and empowerment.

Reaching out for support helps others as well. Giving and receiving aids healing for both the giver and receiver and reminds us of our connectedness with the larger world. The power of giving serves an important role in improving our mood and increasing the desire to keep going on the healing path. To give *is* to receive! Many support groups emphasize that service to others is crucial to maintain their own wellness. So if you feel reluctant to reach out for help, remember that you are actually doing others a favor. Helping you, helps them. When you understand the value of serving others, you will no longer struggle with thoughts of insecurity, embarrassment, or being a burden. Helping others is a two-way street of healing and support.

Layer 1: Feel

Listen. Observe. Honor.

The Conqueress feels with her entire being. Her emotions pulse freely through her veins. She knows no shame in having strong and fierce emotions. She is not afraid to love or be vulnerable. She treats herself with honor and self-compassion. Her mind, body, and soul are strongly interwoven.

*   *   *

In this first layer, you will learn to become mindful and re-establish the mind-body-soul connection and begin to strengthen your vagal tone, allowing you to recover from stress more quickly and improve your emotional stability. Vagal tone is an internal biological process that represents the activity of the vagus nerve; a "higher" vagal tone indicates that your body can recover well after stress. In so doing, you begin to trust yourself to feel the full spectrum of emotions while recognizing that they often come and go. In the moment, strong emotions may feel all-consuming. When you learn that these sensations are fleeting and their intensity occurs in waves, it provides relief. When you allow yourself to simply feel them without judgment, you "hear" the message your body is trying to communicate and then you can respond appropriately and calm the system. You will activate the parasympathetic nervous system and set the stage to rewire your mind and heal your heart. In so doing, you move toward empowerment and begin to restore your confidence, integrity, and sense of self-worth.

My Feelings

I was about four or five years old, the oldest daughter of five children, all born within a six-and-a-half-year span. I remember crying in the family kitchen in an attempt for attention and affection among the chaos. The words still echo in my mind: "Stop crying. You need to be a big girl. Your mom doesn't have time for you; she has all these other kids to take care of." Muted, my crying dissolved and I felt shame. Those words resonated deeply within me, coming from someone I adored and who also had authority. Those words robbed me of the safety and security to be myself; to have a voice, feelings, and opinions; to have an authentic expression of myself. Underneath the layers of emotional and psychic carnage, the tears that I was never permitted to shed, the anger that had to be suffocated, the joy that I never thought I deserved, I had learned to numb, to ignore and discredit my feelings. For some, that situation may have been easily forgotten, but for me it was not. It was traumatic and had a ripple effect throughout my life.

It's important to honor your unique situation or experience. Trauma is based on *your* interpretation of what happened, not someone else's. Trauma isn't defined by the actual event but how you experience it. Honor yourself and remember that regardless of your circumstances or where you are in your healing or journey, your thoughts and feelings matter.

As an adult, I had to learn how to let myself re-experience a vast range of feelings and emotions. To restore the connection between my mind, body, and soul, it was essential to allow my feelings to be felt in their pure, unfiltered form. Feelings and emotions are how the mind communicates to the body what *is* and *isn't* in alignment and what needs to be changed or re-evaluated. Allowing yourself to feel anger, for example, may communicate a boundary that needs to be established. Giving yourself permission to feel disappointment may allow you to evaluate your standards and expectations of others. Acknowledging shame provides an opportunity to learn acceptance and self-love. While feeling such "negative" emotions can be uncomfortable or painful, it is through these messages that we begin to change. As we change and take steps toward self-improvement, we become increasingly empowered.

Over time, I was able to accept all my emotions and thoughts, become curious about them, sit with the most uncomfortable, and honor myself exactly as I was. I remember my therapist once telling me that I had the biggest padlock over my feelings she had ever seen. As you can imagine, the process was difficult, scary, and awkward, but in the end, worth every moment of it. All those years of numbing, whether with alcohol, food or the lack of it, or an obsessive attachment to my mobile phone and social media, had left me disconnected from myself – locked in my lower brain, fighting, flighting, and freezing, and unable to heal. The world I knew had crashed to the ground after The Fall and yet I had to stay strong and accountable for my daughter while suffering heartbreak. My identity as a happily married, suburban wife was gone. I remember pleading out loud, "How am I supposed to feel?"

And I meant it. I was numb and disconnected; I could not process my emotions. Prior to this, my life was governed by how to please others. In my co-dependent relationship, I would judge myself by what others thought or said. I didn't know how – or even want – to have a voice. Every fiber of my being was urging me to block out the painful and ugly realities that were in front of me. I worried only about how society would expect me to respond to all of this.

But deeper down, this way of life was no longer an option. I needed to be in my right mind, make good decisions, and defend myself to honor and protect both me and my daughter. It was time to empower myself and thrive. I could no longer hide. Even if I tried, there was nowhere to hide or anything to hide behind.

For most of my life, I had tried to keep up the facade, making sure everything looked great from the outside, so no one would question what was happening on the inside. It was an illusion I had quickly mastered. From the outside, the only thing missing from my American dream was the white picket fence. Don't get me wrong: we could have had one, it's just that a white picket fence didn't suit our Spanish Colonial-style home, swim-up pool bar, and backyard putting green. By all other external measures, my marriage appeared to be picture perfect. On the inside, though, we were both numbing out in our own way. I had become an expert in putting on a happy smile and sending the message that everything was grand.

As a child, I had become acutely aware of, sensitive to, and in-tune with how *others* were feeling. My reactions and responses were directly correlated to how they wanted me to respond to keep *them* at peace. Today, living with empowerment, alignment, and personal knowing, I keep *my* peace. I feel. I smile. I get angry. I get scared. I get excited. I get nervous. Allowing myself to feel has reassured me that I am exactly as I am meant to be. I discovered that it's emotionally safe for me to be in this world. It is safe for me to have feelings, opinions, and ideas. It is safe for me to make mistakes. It is safe for me to be me. I no longer need to numb or avoid my emotions and feelings. Today, I feel, I get curious, I observe, and I embrace.

Sounds simple, right? I wish it was. Through my own experiences as well as working with others, I became aware of just how much effort many of us make to maintain a facade. We smile on the outside and hold the pain in. We create the illusion that everything is fine, and we may believe it at some level. Yet when we live like this, we lose our essential mind-body-soul connection. We lose our sense of intuition, our ability to change, and the pursuit of self-knowledge. We stop living our purpose.

How to Feel

The two purposes of Layer 1 are to become mindful of our feelings and to calm the nervous system. The tools that science has supported – and that I can attest to both personally and with my clients – for facilitating our ability to become aware of those feelings as well as create a space between a stimulus and our response to it are the following:

- Feel Tool #1: Mindfulness
- Feel Tool #2: Breath
- Feel Tool #3: Meditation

These tools train the body to generate messages that we are safe and free of threats; the tools create a foundation for the restoration of peace and internal homeostasis. They prepare the neurons in our brain for the early stages of neuroplasticity – the ability of our brain to reshape itself in a way that supports positive change.

Changing our thoughts and rewiring the brain begins with mindfulness. To heal our emotions and release the feelings that hinder our empowered self, we first need to become aware of the thoughts and beliefs – both positive and negative – that precede our actions and behaviors. When we develop such awareness and insight, we can begin to heal by forgiving ourselves and others, establishing closure, setting boundaries, making amends, and developing compassion. Healing the mind, body, and soul is essential to empowerment because it allows us to experience vulnerability *and surviving* as well as a chance to recognize the ways in which we wish to change. Breathwork and meditation then activate the parasympathetic nervous system and ventral vagus nerve, which are physiologically critical to the rewiring process. Mindfulness, breath, and meditation must be cultivated and embraced to obtain and sustain our empowerment.

Feel Tool #1: Mindfulness

Mindfulness has become such a buzzword these days; more and more people are priding themselves on being conscious of their thoughts and feelings and their surroundings in a nonjudgmental way. The practice of meditation has also grown by leaps and bounds. Still, many confuse mindfulness and meditation as the same. Mindfulness is the practice of being aware and present in the moment. Meditation is a more formal practice with which to focus on and develop different qualities – including mindfulness.

The practice of being mindful may seem simple, but obligations, hectic schedules, and constant demands on our time can make it incredibly difficult to achieve. Additionally, the skill set needed to become more aware of our feelings can be a bit daunting. To start, mindfulness requires us to be non-judgmental; we must notice when we are being judgmental of ourselves and others – in a nonjudgmental way, of course! Trying not to judge myself for judging myself is, well, a bit perplexing. I've learned it's much healthier to focus on staying in a positive mindset than trying to be non-judgmental in a negative mindset.

Allowing ourselves to feel our emotions requires patience, accepting our experiences exactly as they are, and trusting that life is unfolding exactly as it's meant to unfold. This presents a challenge to those who may have been raised in an unstable home or a home with a lack of structure, because more than likely they are overcompensating with a drive to control or manipulate outcomes, assuming they know what is best. We must take responsibility for our actions and behaviors – blaming others is not permitted. We must also be open to new experiences and creative solutions and allow them to flow.

Finally, a mindfulness practice requires us to be intentional and deliberate with our words, thoughts, and actions, all of which depend on our being aware of both our external surroundings and internal patterns. In short, we must be both open yet focused.

As you can see, mindfulness takes effort. Yet one of the reasons that interest in mindfulness remains so high is because of the vast variety of benefits it delivers. Scientific research repeatedly shows a correlation between a consistent mindfulness practice and improved mental and emotional health: lower rates of depression, stress, and anxiety and higher rates of happiness, well-being, and positive emotional states.[27],[28] Mindfulness meditation also leads to fewer and shorter hospital stays, a stronger immune system, improved pain management, and improved overall physical health and wellness.[29],[30] Science even supports interpersonal benefits such as higher rates of achievement, job performance, and job retention as well as improved relationships, including enhanced romantic relationships.[31],[32]

[27] Sumeet Sood et al., "Effect of Short-Term Practice of Pranayamic Breathing Exercises on Cognition, Anxiety, General Well Being and Heart Rate Variability," *Journal of the Indian Medical Association* 111, no. 10 (October 2013): 662–65.

[28] Paul Grossman et al., "Mindfulness-Based Stress Reduction and Health Benefits," *Journal of Psychosomatic Research* 57, no. 1 (July 2004): 35–43, https://doi.org/10.1016/s0022-3999(03)00573-7.

[29] Daphne M. Davis and Jeffrey A. Hayes, "What Are the Benefits of Mindfulness? A Practice Review of Psychotherapy-Related Research," *Monitor on Psychology* 43, no. 7 (July/August 2012), https://www.apa.org/monitor/2012/07-08/ce-corner.

[30] Marc G Schlatter et al., "Progressive Reduction of Hospital Length of Stay Following Minimally Invasive Repair of Pectus Excavatum: A Retrospective Comparison of Three Analgesia Modalities, the Role of Addressing Patient Anxiety, and Reframing Patient Expectations," *Journal of Pediatric Surgery* 54, no. 4 (April 2019): 663–69, https://doi.org/10.1016/j.jpedsurg.2018.12.003.

[31] Ute R. Hülsheger et al., "Benefits of Mindfulness at Work: The Role of Mindfulness in Emotion Regulation, Emotional Exhaustion, and Job Satisfaction.," *Journal of Applied Psychology* 98, no. 2 (2013): 310–25, https://doi.org/10.1037/a0031313.

[32] Davis and Hayes, "What Are the Benefits of Mindfulness?"

Research has even shown benefits to the physical brain. One of them is increased activation of the left prefrontal cortex (connected to positive emotional states) and decreased activation in the amygdala (fight, flight, or freeze). The results are a greater likelihood of developing behavioral changes and new responses to outside influences.

Mindfulness is simple in theory and clearly good for us, but the practice of it can be really challenging. It is difficult to be conscious of our thoughts and feelings in a nonjudgmental way. It is also counterproductive to be stuck in a negative thought process while practicing mindfulness. Too much rumination, especially if in the form of negative thinking or obsessive worry, will sabotage your efforts. Breathwork and meditation can bring us back to mindfulness when the mind wanders.

Stillness is not the same as the practice of mindfulness or meditation but a necessary condition for achieving them. Stillness is something we desire yet are also deeply afraid of. We long for the quiet within yet are fearful of being alone with ourselves and our thoughts. The vulnerable nature of stillness makes it intimidating. In stillness, we may feel raw and unsettled. Yet it's in stillness that we begin to connect with our Conqueress self. In stillness we begin to hear our soul speaking. In stillness we discover our truths. In stillness you will connect with mind, body, and soul. It is in stillness that our answers reside. When we can move past the discomfort of sitting quietly with our feelings and thoughts, we begin to align with our best selves.

Detaching from the daily distractions of life is necessary to understand the benefits of mindfulness. During my time in India, I was often without internet connection, there were no televisions or tablets. I only had my journal and a pen to write with. For the first time in my life, I had no substantial responsibilities. My daughter was being cared for, I had taken vacation time from work, and I didn't have to worry about laundry, cleaning, or preparing for my next client. Time opened up for me and provided the space for self-exploration that otherwise wouldn't have been gifted. It was eye-opening. I had more mental space, which helped me to become more aware of my thoughts and feelings. I became especially mindful of the negative chatter and self-doubt that frequently surfaced. I noticed how various people and experiences made me feel. I became aware of how my body reacted to fear, to love, and to excitement. I became connected to how my thoughts and emotions governed my actions and behavior. I gained insight into when I needed to be self-compassionate rather than critical. It was an epiphany, a window, a glimpse into mindfulness led me to want more. I realized that the more awareness I have, the more ability I have to change and respond to life in ways that are congruent with my belief system – with who I wanted to be and where I wanted to go.

Feel Tool #2: Breath

I remember an especially dark period in my life. My ex-husband and I had not yet secured supervised exchanges for our two-year-old daughter. I had filed the petition in court, but the slow process made the wait even more gruesome. The idea of supervised visits fueled rage in him that filled me with fear. I remember driving to the police station where we would inevitably have face-to-face encounters as we exchanged our daughter. I was consumed with anxiety because I never knew what to expect. The interaction at the drop-off and imagining the hours of time my daughter would have to spend with an unwell and unstable man evoked a plethora of emotions that I could not process. I had not yet learned – or given myself permission – to feel. I would do anything to repress my emotions.

The Conqueress wouldn't have it. She started to wake from her slumber. My path to empowerment slowly began to open. Still, the intensity and pain of facing the former man of my dreams, father of my child, and best friend – the person I had envisioned spending my life with – were strong. When I looked at my future, he had always been standing beside me. My tendency to see the good in everyone and believe that everything could be restored was a last, desperate attempt to convince my logical brain there was hope. Circumstances had turned him into a stranger, someone whose insides I no longer knew. The confusion, the hurt, and the pain finally forced me to acknowledge that my former life would never return.

The Conqueress unveiled to me that it was time to stop numbing myself and start the process of *feeling*. For the sake of myself, my family, and even my ex-husband, I needed to see with clarity and stop living an illusion. Perhaps it was my strong maternal instinct that finally overcame my fear, allowing the Conqueress to take over and guide me to start my inner work. My love for my little girl kept me in alignment; I found the strength to fight for, set, and defend my boundaries. The Conqueress kept me grounded, connected, and supported. She never wavered. I learned to stop caring about what others thought. I realized that people will always have opinions, but they don't know my soul and haven't walked in my shoes. At the end of the day, I chose to live with my decisions and their consequences, both positive and negative.

The feelings were intense and overwhelming to process. Here I was, feeling a deep love and endearment for someone that I now doubted and whose alliance had been severed. Yet I had to confront it while my daughter stood witness to my actions. I had to learn quickly how to lovingly detach myself from my ex-husband's energy and be true to myself. I had to utilize all the tools in my toolbox to be a model of strength, integrity, and compassion for my daughter's sake and ultimately, my own sake.

In those moments, I noticed that I would literally stop breathing. It was if I held my breath because I was afraid to breathe life. Maybe at some level, I didn't feel that I deserved to breathe or was deeply afraid of what the next breath would bring. Not only would I stop breathing, but I also learned (as I describe below) that when I did breathe, I wasn't doing it correctly. Our breath is our vitality, our life force. It connects the mind, body, and soul. Without it, we cannot survive; and by not breathing fully and with awareness, we cannot thrive.

A simple way to evaluate the quality of your own breathing is put one hand on your chest and the other on your stomach. Close your eyes for a moment and take three deep breaths. Pay attention to which hand is moving and how much: the upper hand on your chest or the lower hand on your stomach. If the hand on your stomach moves more, it indicates that you are breathing with your belly, leading to a more relaxed state. This is a healthier way to breathe. Unfortunately, most people breathe with their chest. Chest breathing is typically shallower and often done through the mouth, which may inaccurately send a signal to our brain that we are under stress, shifting us to fight, flight, or freeze when survival isn't needed.[33] Chest breathing essentially activates the threat response, giving ourselves an artificial tiger in the room. When the body is in this state, the heart cannot heal, and the brain cannot change.

The other important observation to make about relaxation and the breath is the difference between breathing through our nose rather than the mouth. From an anatomic perspective, the nose is built as our breathing tube, while the mouth is our feeding tube – and a back-up breathing tube. Most of our breathing should thus come through our nose. When we do that, it tells the brain that we are calm and sets the initial stages of neuroplastic change.

When we breathe through the mouth, it's usually under duress. From an evolutionary perspective, this is because our ancestor's stressors were primarily physical in nature. To them, stress was running from tigers, jumping across ravines, and climbing mountains. The lower brain is fantastic at activating endorphins to assist in this type of movement and survival. When you exercise,

---

[33] Holly Hazlett-Stevens and Michelle G. Craske, "Breathing Retraining and Diaphragmatic Breathing," in *General Principles and Empirically Supported Techniques of Cognitive Behavior Therapy*, ed. William T. O'Donohue and Jane E. Fisher (New Jersey: John Wiley & Sons, 2009), 166–72.

run intervals, or hike a steep mountain, you are likely breathing through your mouth.

In modern times, though, our stress is much more "white collar" and psycho-emotional in nature. We live in overstimulated societies in which we have expectations and demands so we are constantly coping. When we are late to catch a flight or experiencing technical difficulties, we are likely breathing through our mouths. When we're stuck in rush hour traffic, we are often breathing through our mouth. When asked to give a public speech, you just might start breathing through your mouth.

Stress activates the sympathetic nervous system – the "fight, flight, or freeze" response. Sometimes this is helpful and sometimes it is not. If you need to run faster, escape a fire, or are being chased, it's good to have. In a stressful situation that requires complex thinking and executive functioning skills of the frontal lobes, however, the threat response is not our friend. Instead, we need to calm the system by engaging our frontal lobes, where we find our best thinking and the seat of intuition. The executive functioning skills allow us to modulate and regulate our thoughts and emotions, organize and plan, inhibit impulsive reactions, initiate tasks, and monitor our actions. These are the skills that can overcome the stressors of modern living.

To make this shift and calm your system, simply become more aware of breathing through your nose. Catch yourself throughout the day and become aware of where the breath is coming from. Try to inhale and exhale according to a specific number count – slow in 1, 2, 3, 4, and then slow out 1, 2, 3, 4, – and focus on shifting the breath from the mouth to the nose. This can be done anytime and anywhere. Additionally, there are numerous breathing techniques available online that offer an abundance of benefits. As these practices become habit-forming, your actions and patterns of behavior will begin to change.

Feel Tool #3: Meditation

Meditation is an ancient tradition, still used in today's world, all over the world, to create a sense of calm and inner harmony. Although the practice has ties to many different religious teachings, meditation is less about faith and more about altering consciousness, finding awareness, and achieving peace. As we require a greater need to reduce stress in the midst of our busy schedules and demanding lives, meditation is increasing in popularity. Our desire for peace within has led us back to our wise, ancestral Conqueress methods.

While numerous meditation programs exist, research has indicated no significant outcome differences between them. Much of the literature and research on meditation has been focused on Mindfulness Based Stress Reduction (MBSR) and Transcendental Meditation (TM) because they are the most widespread and therefore easily studied. As long as a meditation utilizes the same components, it will be equally beneficial.

Mediation has been correlated with stress and anxiety reduction, higher awareness of thoughts and emotions (mindfulness), increased attention span, and sharper memory.[34],[35] It can also improve sleep, combat addictions, reduce pain, lower blood pressure, and control cravings.[36],[37] It helps to activate the parasympathetic nervous

---

[34] Fadel Zeidan et al., "Mindfulness Meditation Improves Cognition: Evidence of Brief Mental Training," *Consciousness and Cognition* 19, no. 2 (June 2010): 597–605, https://doi.org/10.1016/j.concog.2010.03.014.

[35] Istvan Schreiner and James P. Malcolm, "The Benefits of Mindfulness Meditation: Changes in Emotional States of Depression, Anxiety, and Stress," *Behaviour Change* 25, no. 3 (September 1, 2008): 156–68, https://doi.org/10.1375/bech.25.3.156.

[36] Sala Horowitz, "Health Benefits of Meditation: What the Newest Research Shows," *Alternative and Complementary Therapies* 16, no. 4 (August 2010): 223–28, https://doi.org/10.1089/act.2010.16402.

[37] James M. Pruett, Nancy J. Nishimura, and Ronnie Priest, "The Role of Meditation in Addiction Recovery," *Counseling and Values* 52, no. 1 (October 2007): 71–84, https://doi.org/10.1002/j.2161-007x.2007.tb00088.x.

system, improve vagal tone, allowing us to change our patterns and behaviors. Meditation activates the frontal lobes which house our executive functioning abilities. As mentioned above, the frontal lobes also happen to be the home of our intuition, allowing us to become more aware of thoughts and emotions. The awareness you achieve during meditation is the key to initiate changes in behavior and cognition, feel connected with our emotions, and improve our wellbeing.

Although there isn't a right or wrong way to meditate, it's important to find a practice that meets your needs and complements your personality. My introduction to meditation and mindfulness is rooted in psychology, neuroplasticity, and spirituality and emerged for me out of my crisis. During that dark period of my life, I needed intervention to manage my stress and anxiety. A meditation practice became the solution. Now I use meditations that encompass, sound, repetition, vibration, movement, and imagery to enhance my ability to change my brain patterns toward empowered living. Ultimately, as with any exercise or hobby, find what works so that you actually do it!

The spiritual appeal of meditation also resonated with me. I feel a sense of comfort and peace when I sit on my meditation pillow near my altar surrounded with pictures, candles, and nostalgic reminders of loved ones. While I have always had a strong sense of the spiritual world, I've also been the personality type that needs to understand the 'why' behind something. This may be a direct result of growing up in an authoritarian household and generation hellbent on appearance and performance. Many of those I interact with in my personal and professional life can relate to a history of being told what to do, not being seen or heard, and never having the freedom to question authority. As an adult, I wanted to know why. It's important to understand why we practice meditation the way we decide and how we can carry these sensations into our everyday life.

Are You Safe?

Many of us associate the basic need of safety as physical. However, emotional safety is also a critical need. One can be physically safe but not feel safe enough to freely express their thoughts and emotions. The implications of not having emotional safety can be just as – if not more – traumatic as lack of physical safety.

At a subconscious level, based on past experiences, you may feel unsafe, unloved, or unsupported. While the logical brain doesn't see any problem, deeper levels of doubt keep us from trusting and functioning in the world as we were meant to. We cannot align with our soul's purpose until we rewire those thought patterns and recognize that our past does not define us and that we do have spaces to feel safe, loved, and supported.

For example, was it safe for you to have an authentic expression of yourself? Were you honored for differences in opinions and feelings rather than shunned away? Were you expected to be seen and not heard? What happened when you made a mistake? Did your family apologize or make amends when they hurt your feelings or wronged you? Were you allowed to cry? Could you voice a different opinion on "big" topics such as politics, sexual orientation, or religion?

A critical goal of the process of transformation is to retrain the subconscious mind to know that it's safe to have feelings and emotions, to be fully known and heard. Your inner child may need reassurance that she is being taken care of and that it's safe to be exactly who she is. This will help calm the nervous system and enable a shift in focus from the primitive lower brain to the higher brain in the frontal lobes.

With a consistent meditation practice, this rewiring becomes embedded, allowing you to overcome fear and anxiety and align with the Conqueress within, to overcome obstacles and flow through life with ease and grace. While your circumstances may not change (at least right away), the way in which you respond to them will.

The meditation I suggest below will allow you to begin feeling safe to have *and* express both emotions and feelings. Although it may seem simple, it is very effective, especially for those who may have struggled to have their basic or emotional needs met as a child. This practice is effective at both the subconscious and conscious level.

To start the meditation, relax the mind and body and recognize that you are safe, both physically and emotionally.

Find yourself in a comfortable, seated position.
Gently close your eyes.
The spine is strong, the heart is soft.
Breathe in and breathe out.
Breathe in and breathe out.
Let go of any tightness or tension.
Become mindfully aware of the body.
The heart rate slows down.
The body softens.
Allow the body to come to a state of ease and peace.
As the body relaxes, notice that the mind slowly follows.
Let go of any thoughts.
Let go of any worries.
Let go of anything that may be occupying the mind.
Allow yourself to come fully and completely into place.
Into this space.
Into this time set aside just for you.
Breathe in and breathe out.
Become mindfully aware that in this moment,
You are safe.
You are loved.
You are nourished.
You are supported.
You are safe. You are loved. You are nourished. You are supported.
Notice the confidence and peace that emerges within.
Allow that sensation to encompass your entire being.
You are safe.

> You are loved.
> You are nourished.
> You are supported.
> In this moment, nothing else matters.
> You are safe, you are loved, you are
> nourished, and you are supported.

From there, depending on the circumstances and my emotions, I move into breathwork practices, followed by some hand and arm movements inspired by my time in India (called mudras) and 'active' mantras and meditations I also learned in India called *kriyas*. These approaches originated in Kundalini yoga, which honors vibration as having sacred meaning. My meditations incorporate sound, repetition, vibration, movement, and imagery – all essential for building new tracks in the brain. I end with a few moments of stillness and silent reflection. The end result is bliss. I feel aligned spiritually, my central nervous system is calm, and I know that all is well.

From my personal experiences and working with clients, there are a few tips that will improve your meditation experience and help to make it a regular practice.

1. First, find an area in your home where you have privacy and stillness. Create a special space such as an Altar using sacred or spiritual possessions, pictures, candles, written affirmations, items from a loved one, or anything that brings you connection and joy.
2. Next, try to meditate the same time each day. The morning is often recommended because it starts your day on a positive note. Once you've activated your frontal lobes and calmed your central nervous system, the Conqueress is ready to go! The other reason I like mornings is that I can cross this off my list by conquering the task right away. How many times have you told yourself you were going to exercise in

the morning and, well, didn't? All day long you may have kept thinking, *I need to exercise later.* That mental chatter and the feeling of overwhelm for another thing to do will create unneeded stress.

3. Be realistic about what will work for you. As a mother and career woman, life can get complicated. I used to set my alarm earlier, for example, but sometimes my daughter would get up just as early or my dog would beg for a walk. I learned not to make a diversion or an excuse to not meditate that day. Do your best to find time to incorporate it into your day. I also suggest a Floor-Ceiling concept; this is particularly helpful for those with unpredictable and busy schedules. The floor level is your minimum. It's designed for days when the alarm goes off late, the coffee maker breaks, your daughter can't find her homework, and you run out of milk for cereal. Now you're thirty minutes late for work. For example, maybe the floor level is a one-minute meditation or three deep belly breaths. Just this will show yourself that you are committed to reinforcing positive habits and preventing feelings of guilt or failure by setting unrealistic goals. The ceiling might be saved for weekends when the kids are with the grandparents and the house is quiet. There is nowhere you need to be and nothing that has to be urgently done. Maybe you meditate for 30 minutes and then follow up with some journaling. On other days, your practice may fall somewhere between the two ranges. Regardless of what life throws at you, adjust accordingly using the floor-to-ceiling range to strengthen your commitment to your practice.

4. If time is a precious commodity for you (as it often is for me), a fifteen-minute meditation may be all you'll need. Fifteen minutes is a sweet spot for maximum benefit. Science tells us it's more effective than seven and just as effective as 20 – 30. However, I do find the more time I spend in stillness, the greater my spiritual connections and feelings of Zen.

5. Finally, don't hesitate to use pre-recorded, guided meditations to bring you into stillness if you find that your mind wanders too much. You can find an abundance of free resources on the internet and YouTube as well as my website, www.DrMarcyB.com. I also enjoy apps such as Headspace and Calm for easy access to guided meditations.

For those of you with minimal exposure to mindfulness or who aren't familiar with developing a breathwork or meditation practice, don't get discouraged. This is a process. Consider starting by just becoming aware of breathing through the nose, then add an affirmation. For example, "I choose Peace", "I believe in myself and trust my own wisdom", "I am loved", and "Everything tends to work out for me". You are building a new foundation; persistence and integrity are more important at this point than speed and intensity. For me, the *Feel* Layer took years of practice and patience and is still a work in process. We are always moving forward, even when we feel we are falling behind; there is always more to be curious about. It's not so much the destination but the road you take to get there.

While it may seem easier to avoid your true emotions or to hide behind the facade, you will lose the opportunity to become empowered and live with intention, truth, and clarity. So take the risk. For me, my Conqueress would not be still. She needed to be heard, to be known, to be loved, to be nurtured. My Conqueress was ready to experience the full range of emotions. She was ready to become mindful. She was prepared to sit with discomfort. She was ready to gain deeper insights into how she truly feels, knowing it would be a liberation.

Layer 2: Explore

Learn. Evolve. Persist.

The Conqueress was willing to look at her past. When she did, she did so with self-compassion and an open mind; dedicated to pursuit of personal growth. She consistently stayed curious about all the happenings in her life, with fierce self-love, curiosity, and perseverance.

*   *   *

As my meditation practices and mindfulness exercises expanded and I began to create more pause in my life, I evolved into a more curious being, eager for change. Now I acknowledged at least a fleeting moment of time between my thoughts and actions. I had created space to make a choice – a space between the stimulus and the response. My brain was prepped to change. I recognize that I have always had choices and that there are always consequences to those choices, both good and bad. Creating that pause, that sacred space, gave me the opportunity to use my higher thinking instead of the reactive part of my brain. I began to use logic and reason rather than a fear-based approach to life.

These skills helped me to gain awareness and get in touch with my emotions and feelings. I could discern what I liked and what I didn't. I could recognize the difference between my beliefs and those that were forced upon me. I had become keenly aware of my values, beliefs, and emotions. The progress was substantial. I could feel again. I knew sad. I knew fear. I knew heartache. I knew happy. I knew joy. I was beginning to come alive.

Through this new avenue of aliveness, the old habits and patterns I had conformed to for most of my life still existed. Conformities had been deeply ingrained in my brain, and my heart had not yet healed. Although it was understandable, it was also very frustrating, and I felt defeated when my actions and behaviors didn't align with my new beliefs or desires. This frustration motivated me to peel the next layer and begin to explore where some of these false belief systems emerged and why they existed. Although it was not realistic for me to evaluate or even have awareness of these patterns as a child, the Conqueress was now ready and equipped to begin to Explore as an adult.

While you begin to Explore in Layer 2, continue to keep an open awareness to Feel as you will ebb and flow often across the two layers. Continue honing your mindfulness tools and create habits that calm the nervous system and activate the vagus nerve. You will become more mindful of what your body is communicating and how the mind is responding. It is critical to build on these practices to create new tracks to train the body and mind to respond to stress and fear in a healthier way.

Also, while beginning Explore in Layer 2, keep cultivating a relaxed body and calm state of mind. Recall that when our muscles are relaxed and our mind at ease, the parasympathetic nervous system and ventral vagus nerve in our frontal lobes are activated, which is where our best and most logical thinking occurs. When we are in distress and fear, we are in "fight, flight, or freeze." In this (lower brain) state, we cannot heal, we cannot learn, we cannot grow. The continued practices of mindfulness, breath, and meditation from Layer 1 open us up to feel our feelings and connect to the Conqueress.

In Explore Layer 2, we start to identify and examine the source of our fear-based messages and false and limiting beliefs. Emotional pain is often the result of underlying issues that need defined and explored. If we continue to push them away or ignore them, the emotional pain and fear persists. Only by recognizing where these damaging beliefs and messages come from and why they exist can we begin to reprogram the messages our mind and body are communicating. When we re-establish that mind-body-soul connection, we start to understand what is really going on behind the thoughts and patterns that activate fear and anxiety.

To unpack your Explore Layer, I offer various types of tools: 30/30/30/30, Brain Retrain, journaling, and mantras. Each of these tools operates under the premise that your past experiences have created your perception, both of yourself and the world around you. We aim to alter this false perception, reshaping the narrative to be properly aligned with your authentic self.

Explore Tool #1: Journaling

I recommend journaling both to release and externalize feelings and thoughts as well as to discover and explore Conqueress dreams, desires, and motivations that may have been hidden from your consciousness. Journaling will allow you to get in touch with your true self as well as serve as a creative outlet.

I've known the benefits of journaling for years and yet, early on, I was a master of task-avoidance when it came to sitting down, pen in hand, and taking the time to write. When I finally did begin journaling, I wish I would have started sooner. Now, if you were to visit my home, you would think otherwise. A carefully selected gold-embossed journal with intricate patterns sits on my nightstand. My floral gratitude journal meticulously matches the ottoman it was placed near. I kept a leather-bound journal at my office desk to accentuate my desk organizer. For years, I staged these pages of future healing as accent pieces throughout my home.

If you don't yet have your own journaling practice, start with something modest, such as writing down a single sentence or a gratitude list. It doesn't matter how you do it; it's important to just start. Once you do, you will likely be amazed at what the body is ready to put on paper and release. All too often, these thoughts manifest and accumulate within the physical, leading to mental chatter and anxiety. When we put them out to the world, it somehow takes away their power to distract and devitalize.

There are many methods and styles of journaling: find one that works for you. Currently, I have a morning and evening journaling practice that has evolved from many different modalities and resources. While it's not always possible to spend as much time as I would like to journal, I do make an intentional effort to spend a few minutes writing both morning and night.

I start my morning journaling with an intention. I used to start with setting goals, but I've shifted to setting intentions, which eliminates my perfectionistic tendencies. Intentions are the attitude and effort you bring forward each day toward achieving your desire. Intentions have more to do with the relationship you have with yourself and others.

Goals, by comparison, are usually black or white, all or nothing. They are very specific and focus on external accomplishments. While goal-setting serves a purpose, shifting your emphasis to intention allows you the grace to experience life as it unfolds. If you haven't achieved your 'goals', you may feel ashamed or unaccomplished. You may also feel discouraged and give up all together. When you set an intention, you will notice the small victories and wins along the way. Intentions help us develop self-compassion while making an effort each day; it is the accumulation of small, deliberate actions that yield lasting results.

In my morning journaling, I set an intention and identify a small step to take during the day to support that intention. This is also a good time to reflect on limiting beliefs or false messages you may be carrying that were programmed in you as a child or that you developed when your emotional needs weren't met. It's important to recognize and declare that these patterns are not your fault; they can be ignored as faulty brain wiring. This awareness increases your capacity to create new and healthy paths congruent with the Conqueress way of authentic living.

Examples of Intention-Setting Journaling:

"My intention toward my physical health is to have a minimum of three minutes and maximum of 90 minutes of physical activity. When my physical body is healthy, I feel great and am able to perform the tasks I desire."

"My intention toward spirituality is to light my candles, pray, and do a minimum of three rounds of breathwork. I can come back and meditate more when time permits. When my spiritual guidance system is strong, I flow through life with ease and grace. I feel purpose and clarity."

"My intention is to focus on gratitude throughout the day. I will become mindful and acknowledge blessings, both big and small. I will share words of thanks with those who have brought me joy. I will smile and acknowledge all that I have."

"My intention to challenge a limiting belief is that when I begin to compare my image to others, I remember that the only valid comparison is to myself from one day to the next. My appearance does not define my worth. I am always worthy of love. To think otherwise is faulty brain wiring based

on my childhood experiences. This is not my fault.
I choose to dismiss those negative messages and
declare for myself that I am worthy."

While morning journal helps start my day with focus and
perspective, I typically spend more time journaling and reflecting
on my day in the evening. Specifically, I use this time to draw closer
to my spirituality and release what no longer serves me.

Devotion (Near)

While studying in Rishikesh, India, a word I heard remained with
me: punya. It was explained to me that punya is a Sanskrit word
that encompasses "merit," "virtue," and "sacredness." Through
acts of *punya*, one is able to connect spiritually and move toward
self-actualization and liberation. *Punya* can be acquired by giving
or being of service, spending time in meditation and prayer, and
honoring your moral compass. Essentially, *punya* is what draws us
nearer to our soul and spiritual guidance.

The closest word I could find that describes *punya* is devotion.
Therefore, when journaling, try a making a list or describe the
occurrences throughout the day that made you feel more devoted
and connected to your soul and spirituality. Although I have a
separate gratitude journal, I often find that the things that evoke a
grateful heart also draws me nearer to God.

Whatever you label it – punya or devotion or something else
that resonates with you – the objective is to become aware of what
draws you closer to your soul and spirituality. This awareness will
increase your tendency to repeat the behavior. For example, when
I first began, I noticed that I felt more spiritually aligned during
my meditations, when listening to Christian contemporary music,
and when I was connecting with others. I realized the value of
including more of these into each day for my emotional and spiritual

wellbeing. After several days of doing this, I became more aware of looking for these spiritual messages throughout the day. Messages are always there; it is up to us to see them. These actions increased my Conqueress confidence and freedom.

Music, meditation, walks in nature, and conversations with friends…that's what works for me, and I encourage you to tune into what works for you. What energizes you, what gets you in the flow state faster? Is it playing a guitar? Is it jogging with a friend? Is it reading your daily devotional? Only you can know, and it may take some trial and error until one day it clicks.

FAR (Fears, Anger, and Resentments)

While my journaling of punya draws me nearer to my spiritually, I also note moments when my thoughts distract me away from the devotion. Often, those distractions are FARs: Fear, Anger, Resentment. By noting these feelings while journaling, I can release them. They are completely debilitating to the Conqueress. The differences between the three are subtle, but by distinguishing them, it may become easier to assess and evaluate their toxicity in your life.

F - Fears represent our anxieties about the future. We worry about things that haven't occurred – the possibility of what we don't want to happen. Our fears are usually derived from the unknown: being fully exposed, making mistakes, potential failure, and even fear of success and how it might change your life's trajectory.

A - Anger is based in the present. It occurs because we do not like or agree with what is happening in our lives at the moment. While it's normal to feel anger, it is more important to note how we respond to anger. Well thought-out and rational responses and solutions can be more effective and soul-soothing than yelling, fighting, or arguing. The more mindful we become of creating time and space between a stimulus and our response, the better equipped we'll be to handle anger in a manner that the Conqueress can be proud of.

Resentments are a bitter indignation resulting from feeling that we were treated unfairly in the past. It is a negative and often persistent emotion that often involves an underlying sense of being wronged by another.

1. To start, challenge the negative emotion. Is it logical and rational or is it emotionally driven and perhaps rooted in a bigger issue?
2. Are your expectations of a situation realistic? What brought up that feeling??
3. Recognize that you cannot change or control others. By sending positive and loving thoughts and emotions, you will greatly reduce your own negativity and lovingly detach from the person or situation for that particular moment.

FAR Examples:

Fear: I worry about future opportunities because I'm afraid of failing. I have persistent negative thoughts that my relationship will end based on a false belief that I am unlovable.

Challenge: These fears are based on false beliefs. The truth is that you are loveable. It is safe for you to make mistakes. It is safe for you to fail and to succeed. The adventure in life is trying.

Anger: I yelled at my children when they disobeyed. I hung up the phone on my sister because she didn't agree with me.

Challenge: These behaviors are not appropriate ways to express anger. Others are entitled to have a different opinion than you. Next time, consider modeling an example for yourself and others by setting healthy boundaries and creating and enforcing clear expectations and consequences for negative behaviors.

Resentment: I have built-up frustration toward my parents for not teaching me coping skills.

Challenge: Your parents did the best they could based on their own childhood and experiences. They provided you with many tools, and you are capable of learning and acquiring new tools as an adult. You cannot change the past; you can only grow and learn from it. By accepting what is, you will move forward with peace and grace.

After journaling on what takes me FAR from the Conqueress, I write or say a prayer or affirmation such as:

> *Please release my negative feelings toward myself and others. Allow me to trust that life is unfolding exactly as it is intended.*
> *Thank you for the experiences that have allowed me to grow. Please help me to release toxic and negative thoughts.*

The Serenity Prayer, written by the theologian Reinhold Niebuhr, also brings a sense of peace and enlightenment to our undesired emotions:

> "God, grant me the serenity to accept the things I cannot change, courage to change the things I can, and wisdom to know the difference."

I often find myself using a portion of a loving-kindness meditations such as:

> "May you and I be happy. May you and I be safe. May you and I be healthy. May you and I be at peace."

Taking time to feel and challenge your negative thought patterns by journaling often yields serenity. When we are in this state of being calm, we won't feel as troubled by life's ups and downs. When we are in a peaceful state of mind, we are quicker to create new brain patterns and lay the tracks to our desired Conqueress destination.

The F-A-R exercise was pivotal to releasing shame I had from my divorce. When I realized I no longer had to carry that burden, the burden of shame, I felt lighter and free. After The Fall, I was full of resentment; negative emotions were bursting at the seams. I was resentful of the past which had caused so much pain; I was angry that my life wasn't going the way I envisioned it would. I realized I was also taking much of the situation very personally when it really wasn't about me. My ex-husband's issues were based on his perception of reality; he was acting according to his own belief system and the conditioning he experienced through his life. While his behavior was unacceptable to me, his actions and decisions were about him, not me.

In addition to feeling rejected, abandoned, and very alone, his actions made me question my worth at a deep, subconscious level. Through my journaling, I ultimately recognized that these feelings were based on faulty brain wiring based on past experiences. None of my ex-husband's actions defined me or my self-worth, just as your self-worth isn't based on how others treat you. You don't have to earn it; you have always been worthy. Others' actions, words, and behaviors have no power to dictate or define who and what you are.

Journaling has been a powerful tool for me, but because those patterns had been engrained for so long, I still have moments of feeling rejected, fearful, or unworthy. When this happens, I offer myself compassion. Those old tracks will always be there, but because I am actively making and enforcing new pathways, it is easier to shift to healthy and desired belief systems. In time, those old tracks will quiet their volume and simply collect dust.

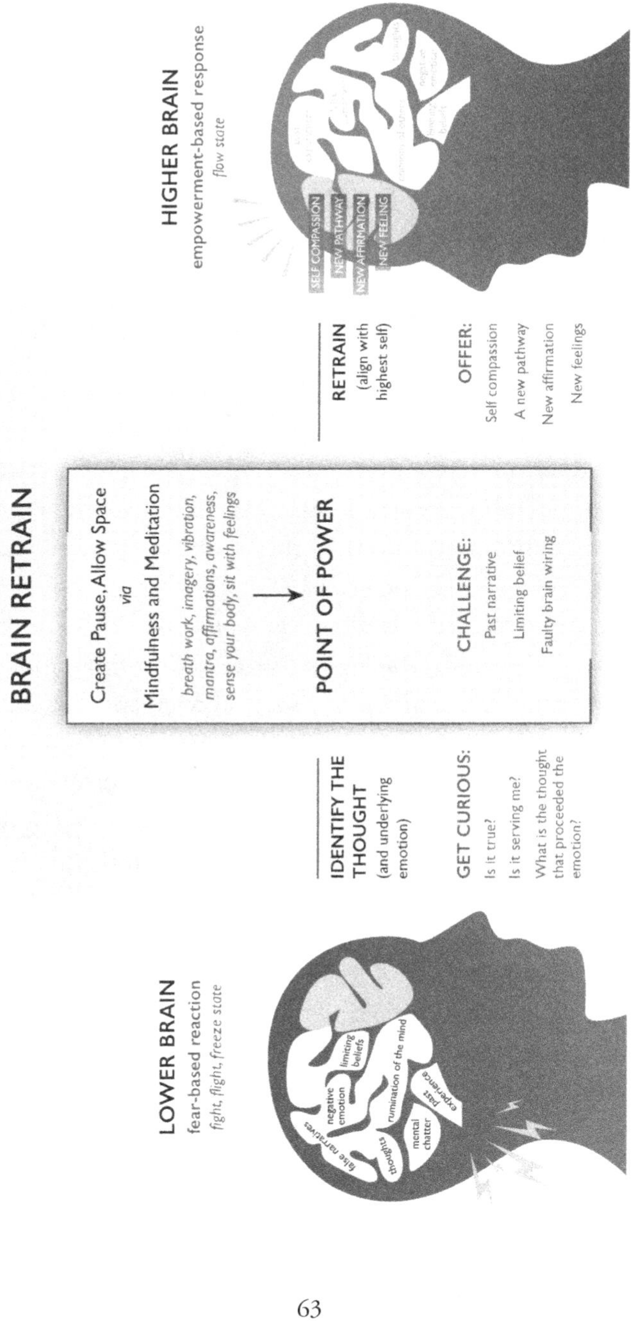

HIGHER BRAIN
empowerment-based response
flow state

SELF COMPASSION
NEW PATHWAY
NEW AFFIRMATION
NEW FEELING

RETRAIN
(align with highest self)

OFFER:
Self compassion
A new pathway
New affirmation
New feelings

BRAIN RETRAIN

Create Pause, Allow Space
via
Mindfulness and Meditation

breath work, imagery, vibration, mantra, affirmations, awareness, sense your body, sit with feelings

→

POINT OF POWER

CHALLENGE:
Past narrative
Limiting belief
Faulty brain wiring

IDENTIFY THE THOUGHT
(and underlying emotion)

GET CURIOUS:
Is it true?
Is it serving me?
What is the thought that proceeded the emotion?

LOWER BRAIN
fear-based reaction
fight, fight, freeze state

limiting beliefs
negative emotion
rumination of the mind
false narratives
thoughts
mental chatter
past experience

Figure 1

Explore Tool #2: Brain Retrain

Take a look at Figure 1. Note that the column on the left is a condensed version of the reactive response from the lower brain. There is little-to-no time for breathing and mindfulness to calm the nervous system. The accumulation of our negative ruminations and mental chatter leads to a lower brain, fear-based response. When you experience a negative emotion or feeling, it is often the mind responding to life based on false, past beliefs. Fortunately, when we identify the feeling and the thoughts that elicit them, we can begin to challenge them and respond differently.

Next bring your attention to the middle column "Point of Power." We are gifted with this space of opportunity when we utilize meditation and mindfulness tools. This is where we begin to rearrange brain patterns: the first step to evolving and growing. While we cannot stop our thoughts and emotions, we do have the power to challenge them and change what we do with those thoughts. Allow yourself to dig deep; realize that this effort can be intimidating and vulnerable to your ego. Yet, in those moments of vulnerability, we can heal and facilitate change and live the life we were meant to live.

The middle column further illustrates how we create the perfect condition for this by continuing to practice the Layer 1 tools for feeling (breathing, meditation, affirmations) and creating more space – a pause – between our thoughts, actions, and behaviors. Those same thoughts, emotions, past experiences, limiting beliefs, and the opinions of others still exist in the higher brain response in the third column. But because you are developing the ability to pause, create space, and clarify, you'll be better equipped to identify their influence. Then you can begin to shift to a proactive and healthier thought process. At the Point of Power, you begin to truly change your brain patterns to align with your Conqueress intentions.

We see how this works in the higher brain response. Notice that the thoughts circulating in the mind are organized in a logical manner. Then the truth of that thought is challenged. Examine past narratives, false messages, and fear-based emotions that may have led to your undesired action. All of these come from past conditioning and brain wiring. It's not your fault.

As you go through this process, be compassionate yourself with words of encouragement, a mindful moment, or comforting your body with a hug, nourishing food, or a warm bath. Again, your past is not your fault. Consider new affirmations to challenge false beliefs and bring you into a space of comfort and peace. In this state, you will have activated your parasympathetic nervous system/ventral vagus and opened yourself to healing and personal growth. When we are operating from this place, we come into alignment with our highest self and create desirable outcomes.

The steps we use to *Brain Retrain* are as follows:

1. Become mindful of your thoughts and emotions. Let go of judgment and simply observe them. What are you feeling? Be sure it is one word: sad, glad, hurt, angry, guilty. It's important to note that fear often underlies many of our negative emotions. We focus on the feeling first because it is the messenger telling us we have work to do. Don't push it away. Acknowledge it. Get curious. This is how we heal.

2. Identify the thoughts and false beliefs that preceded the emotion. When we give them a name, it puts us in charge. We can now take responsibility for our thoughts instead of blaming others. We can begin to challenge these negative patterns once they are identified.

3. The Point of Power when we "retrain the brain" occurs *before* we react to something. Because we utilize mindfulness and apply our Feel tools, we create space and opportunity for behavior change. This is the moment that we introduce choice. Because we are mindful, we have time and

opportunity to make different decisions and determine our actions.

4. Explore and challenge the patterns and conditioning behind those false beliefs. These are faulty messages from the past— usually from childhood – and often a core issue. They often contain the word "should," black-and-white thinking, and irrational beliefs – brain patterns we want to rewire. Create new healthy affirmations to align with your authentic belief system. The goal is to create new, healthy tracks that are congruent with your highest self.

5. Offer self-compassion. Be patient and gentle with yourself and the faulty brain wiring that has been operating. Bring awareness to your dedication and desire to retrain your brain. You are now an adult, working to create a life you love. Your persistence will pay off. All too often, people feel shame, guilt, and failure for their actions. It's likely that your emotional needs weren't met as a child and you are responding from a conditioned pattern. Be proud that you are working to dismiss this faulty pathway and creating new tracks to your desired destination.

Take ownership for your life and actions. Identify your new and desired behavior. Continue to repeat your affirmation to enforce your desire. This is the Conqueress response. In the past, this was likely a fear-based primitive reaction. Our first, and often automatic, reaction to an uncomfortable stimulus is an undesired behavior rooted in past trauma. Remember: Your trauma response is deeply embedded in the fight, flight, or freeze area of your brain, the lower, more primitive part of the brain which is the first part to react. This is important to know because, for a while, you may keep repeating the same patterns over and over. The part of the brain that *remembers* the pain or turmoil of those experiences has no connection with the lower, primitive brain. Meditation and breathwork are the tools that bring logic and reasoning back into the equation.

For example, a lot of my fear-based self-doubt stemmed from a lack of encouragement and validation as a child. I carried a false belief that if others didn't believe in me, I must not be worthy. I also carried a societal misrepresentation that success was defined by appearance, wealth, and fame and a distorted message that a "traditional family" equals happiness. My body would respond with fear, anger, or insecurity to situations where I was expected to perform or fit a particular image. Using the Feel tools in Layer 1, I learned to acknowledge those sensations when they came up. With that awareness, I could now challenge those false beliefs and affirm myself with loving, positive, and accurate messages.

This tool has been a favorite among my clients as well. I recently worked with Maria, who was having a lot of anxiety before giving a presentation at work. She identified her emotion as Fear. From there, we looked for the thought that preceded it. Maria learned that she was afraid of the scrutiny and rejection of others because she would be judged as not good enough. Maria recognized that those thoughts weren't helpful and needed to be changed, so we investigated where that false message may have originated.

We considered past beliefs, and she shared with me that, as a child, her parents rarely gave her positive feedback or attention when she did well. However, if she struggled with a school assignment or her piano performance, they were quick to scold her and make her feel isolated and rejected. She felt that she could never earn their approval. She had taken on the false belief that her worth was dependent on her performance, and that the expectations for her to exceed were unrealistically high. This pressure was highly anxiety-producing because parental approval is crucial to how a child measures their value.

The result: She was always trying to earn her parents' validation, which in her mind she never attained. This caused her to become very anxious before any type of performance no matter how well-prepared she was because she was always afraid of not being validated. Even after a successful presentation, she would isolate and verbally beat herself up for not doing better or more. Her personal life also suffered, and she struggled to maintain relationships.

To break out of this pattern, she needed to challenge the thought. I asked her how she would respond to her child after a piano performance. She said she would hug him and compliment him. I asked how she would respond if he had missed a few notes. She said she would still be proud and tell him that it was okay to make mistakes. I invited her to re-parent herself in that same way – to go back to her own inner child and provide the same words and emotions.

We wrote a script and incorporated affirmations and mantras to remind her that she was worthy and lovable *all the time* and that her value is never defined by a performance. One of those mantras was, "It is safe to be exactly as I am. I am worthy of love all the time." We acknowledged that even mistakes are part of the learning process and need to be acknowledged as just that. Maria read her scripts and used her mantras while setting aside a few minutes before and after each presentation to meditate and process the emotions and thoughts. Using these tools, she was able to shift from having fear and anxiety before a performance to being proud to share her work. She even became receptive to feedback and constructive criticism. She had learned to empower herself by changing her past.

Another client was challenged with food addictions and an eating disorder. We worked together and created the following two narratives based on the Brain Retrain:

> "My thought of needing just one more bite is a sneaky lie. It always leads to more. It puts me at risk of eating addictive foods and sabotaging my recovery.
>
> This delusional thought comes from faulty brain wiring based on my childhood experiences. My emotional needs were not adequately met, and as a result, I used food for comfort. These urges are my brain seeking a way to get a "hit." It is

faulty wiring and false messaging. The truth about having one more bite is that it leads to weight gain, depression, shame, and lack of integrity. It robs me of peace. I can disregard these thoughts and remind myself that I am a grown woman who doesn't have to respond. My food addiction is not my fault. My eating disorder is not my fault. I release all guilt and shame from it. I offer myself compassion and love. Today, when the urges come, I will reach out for support, breathe, take a walk, and drink tea. By following my recovery plan and trusting it is enough, I can relieve myself of mental chatter and self-doubt. In doing so, I am creating a life that I am proud of."

"Today, I feel anxious and recognize my thoughts to eat extra food when I am home alone. In the past, food was a distraction for the stillness and quiet. Eating kept me 'busy.' Today, I choose to embrace the quiet as a time to engage in self-care and to connect with myself. As a child, I received the false message that I had to be productive to be worthwhile. And so I turned into a human-doing instead of a human-being. As a result, my mind challenges me when my body and soul want to relax. I can recognize this as faulty wiring. I will challenge those thoughts and offer myself compassion for all the times I could not discern the difference. I release all shame and guilt. When I feel these thoughts come, I will recognize them as false messages. Instead, I will embrace my "me' time and allow myself to relax. I will take a bath, drink tea, reach out for support, and meditate. I will focus on gratitude and self-compassion. The reality of eating for comfort has always been discomfort. I choose to challenge this false message and live a life I love. I deserve to be happy, thin, and free."

The Brain Retrain tool does take a bit of practice, but over time, you will begin to process the steps relatively quickly. You will become more mindful when a specific feeling comes up repeatedly, or you experience the same reactions. You can then identify the feeling and immediately shift to your affirmations and mantras. So rather than react to a negative feeling of failure, for example, you simply remind yourself that it's safe to make mistakes and that you are lovable all the time.

You can also become proactive with these tools. When you know you're about to encounter a situation or event that may elicit a specific uncomfortable feeling, you can take preventive measures by utilizing the affirmations and mantras ahead of time to minimize and even eliminate any irrational and undesired thoughts. Identify the feeling and immediately respond, shifting your chatter to positive and helpful instead of negative, via your affirmations and mantras. When working on ourselves, sometimes the hardest part is to start. Maybe you have a whole stash of tools but rarely pull them out. Taking a deep look at yourself is a courageous act. But once you do, you will be grateful and wished you would have done it sooner!

Explore Tool #3: Mantras / Affirmations

Perhaps you have dreams, ambitions, desires, and goals that you just can't seem to reach. Negative thought patterns are also working against yourself. Your own mind is working against you. You become accustomed to fear-based and reactive patterning and start to believe that you will never reach your goals. Fortunately, you are designed to experience peace, purpose, and prosperity. You are designed to be an empowered Conqueress.

While each of the tools in the Feel layer build stronger neural pathways to our intuition and highest self, the consistent use of tools for Explore create the space for change to happen and also help to reprogram the brain. When you get into the habit of repeating healthy and desirable mantras or affirmations, you start cutting through the negativity with positive energy. Over time, this constant mind loop of "I'm not good enough" or "I'm not deserving" or "This is too hard" are replaced with words of confidence, peace, love. The vibration of that good energy keeps reverberating at a subconscious level.

You may notice that I have used the words *mantra* and *affirmation* interchangeably, but there are important differences in psychology, science, and spiritual literature. I will share below what those differences are to me in hopes that it inspires you, or at the very least, encourages you to define what it means to you, too.

Mantras

Mantras are a powerful tool when it comes to rewiring the brain and increasing the vagus nerve connection. Mantra is derived from Sanskrit *man-* "to think" and *-tra* meaning, tool, Thus, they literally mean "instrument of thought." Mantras are words or phrases repeated to calm the mind, promote spiritual growth, and bring awareness. The earliest mantras are believed to have originated in India over 3,500 years ago. Using a mantra repeatedly activates the vocal cords and the muscles in the back of the throat. The immediate effect is toning the vagus nerve and activating the parasympathetic nervous system.

The benefits of mantra expand beyond that, for example, helping us to focus and settle our minds. As we go through our day, most of us tend to have very negative mental chatter. We live in a society of judgments, pressure, inadequate coping skills, and unhealthy patterns and conditioning. Most of this is negative – whether or not it's true – but our minds constantly react to it all. If you were to go through an entire day and write down everything you say to yourself, you would probably be shocked!

"I'm not good enough." "I'm not smart enough." "They don't like me." Even though we may not say these out loud to ourselves, the thoughts and emotions behind them arise. You may notice this in feelings of insecurity, fear, lack of ambition, and self-doubt. Beyond those are the other things we tell ourselves that further hinder our happiness. "I'm bored." "I can't do this." All of these things have a negative effect on our emotional and psychological wellbeing.

My understanding of mantras surfaced during my time in Rishikesh, India. This was a very healing, insightful, and profound experience for me. Rishikesh is known as the birthplace of yoga and home to many ashrams and sacred communities where people flocked to spend time in stillness. The songs of the famously popular Beatles release, the "White Album," was written at an ashram I visited there. Numerous other celebrities have gained mental clarity and peace in these humble and sacred spaces. You can feel the spiritual energy as soon as you enter.

It was within these walls that I practiced *kriyas* – a Sanskrit term for "action" used within yoga practices to achieve a specific result. Each *kriya* has an intended purpose, such as releasing fear or experiencing joy. These specific techniques are described as tools for transcending the mind. They utilize repetition, sound, and vibrations that help you enter a deep state of meditation. Their meanings are eloquently summarized in just a few words. Mantras are often falsely perceived as having a religious origin when they do not. Although some religions, including Buddhism, may use Sanskrit, Sanskrit itself is not a religion. It is a language in which some of the words describe ideas and actions that have the power to calm our nervous system and activate our highest and best thinking.

What I love about these Sanskrit mantras is that they contain many of the concepts used in science and psychology to activate the vagus nerve and rewire our brains. Think, for example, of the sound of "Om" and how it resonates in the body as you chant it in yoga or prayer. That vibration is essentially activating the vagus nerve and our frontal lobes, calming our systems and allowing clear thinking while also representing profound and beautiful meaning. Some of the mantras I've used include:

Aham Brahmasmi – *I am, unity, as I give, so do I receive.*

Aham Prakasha – *Waking up to the light within, I am Light.*

Om – *The sound of everything and nothing, Oneness*

Om Shanti Shanti Shanti – *Oneness peace, peace, peace.*

Hari Om Tat Sat – *All is one and of the truth.*

Sat Chit Ananda – *Truth bliss consciousness.*

Aham Prema – *I am Love.*

So Hum – *I am, I am that, that I am, connecting with oneself with the universe or ultimate reality.*

Om Namaya Shivaya – *I surrender my lower self to my true self; I die to all ignorance so that I may be born anew; I recognize the fierce presence of freedom within me. I bow to that.*

Om Mani Padme Hum (mantra of the Bodhisattva of compassion) – *Let the sacred jewel of my lotus heart shine forth and bring Light and joy to the world and me.*

The use of mantras also affects our meridian points. Meridian points are found within the peripheral and central nervous system

which, when stimulated, provide information to the brain.[38]
Acupuncture, which is regarded as the primary treatment in Ancient eastern medicine, was developed from the system of meridians. When you chant or repeat a mantra, the tip of the tongue stimulates energy points on the roof of your mouth that activate your hypothalamus. This stimulates your pineal gland ("the seat of your soul") and your pituitary gland and is like a tonic for the entire glandular system. There are tremendous scientifically proven healing benefits to repeating mantras.

Affirmations

Affirmations are positive statements that challenge and overcome self-sabotaging and negative thoughts. Affirmations typically include "I Am" statements:

- I am brave.
- I am confident and tenacious.
- I am on a journey, always evolving and growing.
- I am radiant.
- I am accepted and supported.

---

[38] John C. Longhurst, "Defining Meridians: A Modern Basis of Understanding," *Journal of Acupuncture and Meridian Studies* 3, no. 2 (June 2010): 67–74, https://doi.org/10.1016/s2005-2901(10)60014-3.

Figure 2

Think of Maslow's "hierarchy of needs." As rudimentary as it may sound or feel, we need to re-establish a solid foundation of safety and security in order to attain "self-actualization" – the top of Maslow's pyramid. At a cognitive and conscious level, we are aware that we are physically safe. Yet when we are in distress and the lower brain is activated, our subconscious and reactive responses kick in. In this state, memories stored by our subconscious brain as being emotionally or physically unsafe may get triggered. Stop, and rewire those neural pathways. Teach yourself that regardless of your childhood experiences, you are worthy of respect, you are entitled to have a voice, to have an opinion, and have an authentic expression of yourself. It is safe for you to make mistakes without jeopardizing your worth, values, and respect. As you build more security and safety into your life, you will notice a shift to feelings of belonging, love, self-esteem, and self-actualization.

Affirmations that start to re-establish a sense of security and a foundation for the subconscious mind to 'feel' safe can include:

- It is safe to have feelings and emotions.
- It is safe to express myself.
- It is safe to set boundaries.
- It is safe to make mistakes.
- It is safe for me to feel my emotions.
- It is safe for me to be fully known.

While the benefits of using positive affirmations have been established, it's important to note that using them can be counterproductive if you are clinically depressed or feel a level of disconnect or lower self-worth when using them. To work with these issues while using affirmations, I suggest the following process.

For example, let's say the affirmation you are using is "I am strong" but in the moment you are not feeling very strong.

1. Acknowledge that you don't feel strong and that's okay.
2. Recall a time when you did.
3. Reflect on that experience and those emotions.
4. Acknowledge that even if you aren't feeling strong in the moment, it doesn't mean that you don't possess the capability to do so.
5. Bring those past experiences of when you did feel strong into the present moment.

It would go something like this. "Right now, I'm not feeling strong, but I remember when I did feel strong. I felt confident and proud. I remember when I stood up for myself and faced adversity. I felt very strong at that moment. In fact, the more I think about those experiences, the more I feel that strength coming back. Yes, I am strong! I'm aware that even when I don't notice my strength, I am still strong. The more I do notice this, I will know that I am strong. I. Am. Strong.

Explore Tool #4: 30/30/30/30

We know that repetition is key for encoding information into the brain as well as re-training the subconscious mind. Each of our senses house a receptor cell that becomes stimulated by various forms of energy. It then sends an electrical signal to the part of the brain assigned to process that corresponding sensation. Additionally, the more senses we utilize in this encoding (i.e., sight, sound, touch), the higher the signal, therefore the greater likelihood of the message being received by various receptors. The 30/30/30/30 tool, to be done for a period of thirty days, is designed to support your effort to develop a new habit or make a behavior change.

First, pick a mantra or affirmation and write it down 30 times. Then, using some type of recording app or device, repeat it out loud 30 times. Then, listen to yourself declare your affirmation

30 times. Do this every day for 30 days and incorporate the same affirmation as much as you can throughout the day. While repetition is key to this tool, if you feel intuitively guided to change the affirmation or mantra throughout, trust your guidance system. Try setting an alarm on your phone to repeat the mantra and/or write and post the affirmations in places where it will be easy to see. For example, I've posted mine on my steering wheel, my refrigerator, and my mirror.

When utilizing this tool, affirmations should always be stated in the positive. For example, instead of "I won't yell at my kids," you would say, "I am peaceful and calm when I approach my children." The brain processes words whether they are positive and negative – it's much better to say "want" and "will" and "don't" and "won't." Have you ever told your children to "Don't run!" and it doesn't have much effect, maybe makes it worse? This is because the brain hears and processes the word "run." Better to say, "Please walk," to slow down the pace. The same thing happens in our brain. To stop an undesirable behavior, we must find a replacement for it. So, by positively stating our desired action and behavior, we train the brain to respond accordingly.

Can you relate to growing up in an environment where it wasn't acceptable to be authentic, to be fully known or heard, to laugh freely, to make mistakes without criticism, to have opinions that differed from your family, to take an honest look? Was it safe to have emotions? Was it safe to feel? Was it safe to have a voice? If not, those roots run deep, and you'll need to retrain yourself at a deep, subconscious level.

As you prepare for 30/30/30/30, choose an affirmation that intuitively belongs to you. You will know when it feels right. Don't question or doubt yourself. Here are some examples of "progressive" affirmations similar to those I have followed. Remember: Only focus on one affirmation at a time for the 30-day period.

- Peace, love, and abundance are always available to me.
- I choose healing/recovery.
- I love and accept myself exactly as I am.
- I love and respect my body.
- I trust that life is unfolding exactly as it is intended.
- I am healed. I am recovered.
- I am Love.

Layer 3: Acceptance

Pray. Trust. Thank.

*T*he Conqueress takes wise risks. She has a keen sense of what parts of her life are within her ability to control and which ones Mother Nature and the universe are better equipped to handle. She acts with confidence and poise when needed. She lets go with grace and trusts when her intuition directs her to do so. These skills have been lost in the hustle and bustle of the modern world. Somewhere along the way, humankind developed the distorted idea that we were in control, that we held the pen to write our future. The Conqueress knew that there was no such pen. She simply relied on the interconnectedness of her mind, body, and soul.

*   *   *

The Acceptance Layer amplifies spiritual discernment. In Layer 1, you re-established the connection between your mind and body by listening to your feelings and the messages your body was sending. In Layer 2, you explored why and how previous beliefs and conditioning have impacted your responses to life's many and varied encounters. For Layer 3, the Acceptance Layer, the influences will be further broken down and psychologically – as well as spiritually - explained. In order to effectively balance the mind, body, and soul, priority and attention must be given to our spiritual wellbeing. For many, meditation practices can lead to more spiritual awareness and clarity.

Spiritual discernment is more than just a process or a skill. Even in the most mundane or meticulous matters: there is a spiritual force working for our benefit. The voice of intuition is often nudging us, leading us, and supporting us. In matters of our mind and body, there are methods, processes, lessons, and tools which our spiritual self can work through to help us discern correctly. Spiritual discernment isn't usually a sudden zap from beyond but something that emerges from mindfulness and close attention. Eventually, you become more open to accept "what is" is there for your benefit even when it's beyond your understanding or even your liking. Acceptance of "what is" helps you to see through facades and confusion, enabling you to get to the heart of the matter. As you continue to build on your mindfulness practice of non-judgmental observation, you can also begin to build acceptance about those observations.

Spiritual discernment through acceptance can guide your next steps of action. By listening for that nudge or internal source of guidance, you feel reassured in moving forward. Be mindful, too, that doing nothing is an action as well. This can be either good or bad. For example, are you not taking action based on fear or because your intuition counsels patience? If the prior, go back to the Point of Power to learn how that faulty message occurred and then rewire that brain pattern into one that aligns with your highest self. If you aren't taking action because intuitively you feel compelled to be still - listen. Perhaps it's a task for another or not the right direction for your journey. Simply Trust.

Acceptance, then, is about both taking action and allowing deep surrender. This is where spiritual discernment comes in: having a trust, a confidence, that something more powerful and more loving than you can fathom has *your* best interest at heart. Knowing this humbles me and also gives me relief from my otherwise relentless tendency to plan and orchestrate life. I can breathe, I can smile, knowing that all will be okay – even better than okay. Knowing that there will be an epic and exact solution for my heart's desire and my soul's purpose. Again, these tools take effort and practice, and you may benefit from getting some extra support. Be gentle and loving with yourself as you ebb and flow in the journey of learning how to discern your inner guidance system.

The ability –and the willingness – to surrender and relinquish control can be challenging. Control has often been described as an illusion; we like to believe we have control of things like which job we get, who we marry, and how our kids will behave. As a result, we find ourselves trying to manipulate or control situations and people. All to get what we think we want. In truth, the only thing we have control of are our own actions.

Our thoughts will come and go as they please. The same is true with our emotions. We don't have the ability to decide which thoughts pop up or how we are going to feel about them. We can take action steps such as meditating, using affirmations and mantras, and finding a therapist to increase the chance of generating healthy thoughts and emotions instead of negative ones. Ultimately, thoughts do what they do. The more we continue to create space and acknowledge our thoughts and emotions, the greater the opportunity to make rational choices, how to better respond to those thoughts. A thought can be just a thought. Observe the thought, acknowledge the feeling and get curious about the emotion, and decide to release the thought if it doesn't serve you. You have the power and permission to release a thought or act on it as you see fit.

Now, take a few deep breaths and allow your thoughts to just flow.

- What areas of your life are you attempting to control?
- Is that effort serving you?
- What is holding you back from letting go and surrendering?

Fear can keep us from manifesting our greatest desires, achieving our highest potential, realizing our deepest purpose, and being the person we were created to be. Now that you have the tools and resources to start living a fearless life, I invite you to take a few moments to reflect and write down what that life will be like when you let go of the fear of failure, of judgement, of rejection. What will you do? Where will you go? Who will you be? When we live with trust instead of fear, we are aligning with our highest selves. It's there, in that place, where we achieve our greatest joy, fulfillment, and peace. Take a few moments to reflect, write, draw, or simply imagine the life that is waiting for you. Then close your eyes and see yourself in this new role feeling confident, proud, and strong.

As you work through this layer, it's important to remember that neither life nor healing is a linear process. Linear thinking functions well for some things, for example, balancing a checkbook. Ten plus ten will always equal twenty. A gas tank must have gas for the car to run. Good grades are a prerequisite to getting into a good college. The list of linear thinking presents the black and whites, the always consistent elements of life where one thing leads to a specific outcome. Most of life, however, does not operate in the same way. Holding on to life, wishing it were linear, trying to compel aspects of your life towards a straight line will assuredly lead to frustration, depression, and despair. For me, meeting someone special, getting engaged, and getting married did not lead to "happily ever after." Graduating from college, applying for a job, and getting an interview does not always lead to an actual job.

Life is cyclical. When we become mindful that there are ups and downs, ebbs and flows, and truly believe that life is happening *for* us, we can accept any experience with ease and grace. Whenever you feel doubtful, remember what you've been learning. Step back and look at the bigger picture. Acknowledge your wins! Resist the urge to let even one perceived 'failure' or slip backwards outweigh the progress you have made. Focus on what is working and remember that every experience is an opportunity to heal and grow. When we let go of the illusion that specific actions yield specific results, we begin to humble ourselves and let go of the ego. We get out of our own way. This is when true healing occurs.

Action Steps

Prior to The Fall, I was happily living in a suburb surrounded by traditional family trappings. After The Fall, with a drastically different heart, I became mindful of all the couples and families as I visited the same events, restaurants, and shops I had in the past. I felt as though I was the only single parent. Most of my friends were married with children. My dating options were limited within a twenty-mile radius. I was a single parent living in an area that no longer coincided with my identity.

As a naïve farm girl, I had always longed to experience city life, yet I was intimidated by it. I needed a fresh start, a new beginning, and now was the time. My daughter would be starting kindergarten and it was important to keep her enrolled in the same school to maintain stability and consistency.

Stepping out of my comfort zone felt scary, but by now, I knew I could do hard things. My Conqueress courage and determination pulsed through my veins. I knew the prestigious area of the city where I wanted to live and where I wanted my daughter to attend a well-respected school. It was expensive, but I was willing to make sacrifices.

I have always loathed the quote, "Everything happens for a reason," Not that it's untrue. I do believe it. I just feel that it's often used as a cop-out for justifying the natural consequences of an action. It is the beginning of an explanation that is rarely finished. By failing to complete that sentence, we also fail to acknowledge the true reasons and consequences of our choices.

For example, I remember when a peer got pregnant in high school. Instead of acknowledging that her pregnancy was the result of having unprotected sex, members of the community ignored that reality and simply proclaimed, "Everything happens for a reason." Or when I didn't make the cheerleading team because I had never been trained or practiced. I was told, "Everything happens for a reason." This may be true, but it was also true that I didn't make the squad because my skills weren't adequate compared to others who spent years taking classes to become prepared for the tryouts.

Moving to the city wasn't going to miraculously happen. If I wanted this experience, I needed to act on it. I began taking drives to the city and exploring. I began looking for rental apartments. I applied for several jobs in the area. I was offered four positions and knew immediately which one I wanted. I prayed. When fear surfaced, I decided to experience excitement instead. The reason I was able to move to the city, get a new job, move to a new apartment, and enroll Elyse in kindergarten is because I took action.

There comes a time when you have taken all the possible action steps and it's time to invite surrender. I recognized this as I took those steps toward my envisioned move. I had done all I could do; my checklists were crossed off. If my path didn't take me in that direction, I was willing to surrender and accept that the suburbs were a better place for me. Yet I wouldn't have been able to get to this point if I hadn't actively stepped toward my vision. Only then, did I find deep surrender and turn the outcome over to a force greater than me.

Acceptance Tool #1: Change the Way You Pray and Ask

I was the girl with the plan for my life. I would go to college and get a degree. I would meet the dream guy. We would travel and have romantic excursions before we got married and had two kids. I would get a corporate job and wear designer shoes with my sophisticated black suits. We would have a housekeeper and a pool boy. We would wear matching sweaters for our family photos and red flannel pajamas at Christmas while we sat in front of a glittering tree, opening gifts. However, that plan only existed in my mind. Looking back, it was so far from my reality that it makes me laugh. Yet when I really stop to think about it, my life may not 'look' the way I thought it would, but my desired outcomes of family and belonging, financial stability, connection and companionship, are all present in my life today. By letting go of how you think life is supposed to appear and releasing the notion that you have all the answers, you may find that you get to where you want to be with much more ease and grace.

If you grew up in an emotionally unstable home, you may have learned to apply intense control to every area of your life, relentlessly trying to create a sense of stability. As my ego dissipated and the Conqueress revealed herself in my life, I began to change my prayer and let go of what I thought *should* happen. I recognized that *my* way may not always be the best way or even good at all. I learned to trust something greater than myself. The method doesn't have to be traditionally religious, although it can be.

Prayers or requests often go something like this:

- "God, please help me win the competition."
- "I want to get pregnant. Please help me."
- "Please help me to find a date for my friend's wedding."
- "Please help me get the job I want."
- "Please help my kids to do well in school."

We tend to get very specific about what we want. And while it's okay to be specific, when we remember that we don't have control of outcomes, we are setting ourselves up for potential disappointment. Instead, I invite you to focus on the sensations or qualities that are related to what it is you think you desire. For example, praying for a job that provides financial stability, a sense of purpose, and flexibility for family will open up more opportunities than if you focus on the idea that a specific job is best. In that way, you expand your request to finding any job with those qualities. Trusting that outcome will give you peace. Perhaps more importantly, in relinquishing the need to control, you will allow your Conqueress's purpose to begin to manifest. As I began changing the way I prayed, what I prayed for changed as well:

- The strength and wisdom to carry out my purpose.
- The ability to accept life on life's terms.
- To ability align with my highest self.
- To be both empowered and supported.
- To heal my mind, body, and soul.
- To release my ego.
- To have complete trust and gratitude for my life as it unfolds.

We start to release control when we change how we ask and what we ask for. Releasing control *is* surrender. Surrender literally means to stop fighting; Stop fighting with yourself. Stop fighting the universe and defying the natural flow of life. Stop resisting and pushing against reality. When we experience this true surrender, we come to have complete acceptance of "what is" and trust that all is well.

The lifted weight and released burden will leave you in awe. You will probably ask yourself, "*Why did I keep myself on such a tight leash for so long?*" The truth is that most of us have very strong willpower and egos, often as the result of childhood trauma such as parental instability, a lack of attention and affection, or being deprived of emotional or physical security. As a defense, we try to control and manipulate. It's how we survived: defense mechanisms. Even after we have gleaned the benefits of surrender, we can find ourselves trying to control again. Don't despair! We are rewiring the brain and creating new and healthier neuropathways. It's only normal to revert back to old patterning from time to time. That's why I encourage you to journal your experiences with surrender so you can look back on your progress.

Think back over the course of your life towards those moments that hit you the hardest when you were disappointed. Can you start to see that life was happening *for* you, even though what you "thought" was best at that time did not come to fruition. This is another good journaling exercise: focusing on the gratitude you now have for that unanswered prayer.

It is helpful to recall these past events in current moments of pain and anguish when we are struggling with the illusion of what we think is best for us. Maybe it was a relationship that ended against your wishes but now you have found someone much more compatible. Now, you look back and see how the past relationship wasn't serving you even though it was so hard to admit at that moment. Maybe you didn't get into the field of study you applied for but found a profession that is much more rewarding.

Constantly remind yourself: Don't get attached to outcomes. The illusion of control, the idea that we know what is best, is a trap: I want this job. I will get married. I want a baby at a particular age. I need to get accepted to this university. Instead, I invite you to focus on the *why's* behind your desires rather than a particular outcome. For instance, instead of being hyper-focused on the director position at an elite agency, be open to what will align with your heart's desires. You don't actually know if that job will give you what you want, so focus on what you do know. If you want a job that provides financial security and family flexibility, that challenges and motivates you, that allows you to contribute meaningfully to society, it may not be at an elite agency so be open to the possibilities. When we make our requests in this mind-frame, we invite opportunities and scenarios that we may never have considered or thought possible.

After my morning meditation, I recite the following daily prayer:

God,
I offer myself to you, to build with me
and do with me as you see fit.
Relieve me of my ego, that I may better serve Your Will.
Support and guide me through my difficulties
so I may begin to view them as opportunities and blessings.
Throughout the day, God,
allow my thoughts to be Your thoughts,
my words to be Your words,
and my actions to align with those of Yours.
My one simple prayer, my one humble request, God,
is for the strength and willingness to carry out
your Will,
your purpose,
your plan
for my life,
with deep, deep gratitude
and
deep, deep trust.
Amen.

Acceptance Tool #2: Change Your Perception

Blinders

Without the guidance of my Conqueress, I would tend to get very attached or fixated on my goals. All I could see was whether I had maintained my weight, got a 4.0, won the competition, fit into the dress, got the promotion, made my parents proud, bought the car, had a date for the wedding, passed or failed. I was either successful or I wasn't. My world was black and white. Because I am fierce and strong-willed, I worked diligently to meet my goals. When I didn't succeed, I was devastated – a complete failure.

From past conditioning, my survival, self-acceptance, and sense of self-worth depended on the outside perception that I was "okay." Meeting my many standards "proved" that I was good, that I had it all together. Observed from the outside, it would certainly look that way. Inside, I was so controlled by those external perceptions and my own projections. Inside, I was numb with no connection to my emotions. With my blinders on, it was all or nothing: I was lovable or I wasn't. I was successful or I wasn't. I was skinny or I wasn't. I was smart or I was a mockery.

During my healing journey, that external locus of focus shifted inward. I cared far less about what others thought and started directing much more compassion toward myself. The legitimacy of my thoughts, my ideas, and my self-worth was at stake. I started focusing on nurturing, befriending, and connecting my mind, body and soul. Rather than struggle to achieve what or how I thought I should be, I just accepted and allowed myself to be "as is." During this process, I had unintentionally and inadvertently removed my goal-driven blinders. Rather than living in black and white, my life became a silvery happy medium, a pearly grey.

With the removal of these dark, bulky blinders, I could finally see! I could see the journey and the bigger picture. I could see the growth. I could see the healing. My self-compassion and self-love expanded exponentially. I became gentler and more accepting of myself and others. When we stay in a state of self-criticism, beating ourselves up and engaging in self-deprecating habits, we will never arrive at where our highest self wants to go. So, take off those blinders and celebrate the wins, no matter how big or small. Acknowledge and embrace your progress!

Lenses

In addition to blinders, we have several lenses through which we view ourselves and others. When children experience emotional trauma or neglect from a parent or authority figure, the result is often feelings of low self-worth and insecurity. Parental relationships are experienced by a child as the most meaningful and accurate representations of their value. Both positive and negative beliefs about themselves as influenced by the parents are absorbed. These perceptions become the lens through which they begin to see themselves as well as others. The impact of negative experiences can lead to self-criticism, self-punishing, or self-harming behaviors, shame and guilt, and ignoring basic emotional needs.

As I became more mindful of my own self-critical and perfectionistic tendencies and began to transform them into healthier and more accurate perceptions, I also became aware of my outlook toward others. In general, I am mostly judgmental only to myself, whereas I have compassion for others and realistic expectations. Yet in my own personal romantic relationships, especially if they were becoming more serious, I noticed that I often became very judgmental. I was afraid of rejection, and given the trauma of The Fall, my unhealthy attempt at self-preservation was to see relationships through a distorted and damaged lens.

After my marriage ended, whenever I met someone new, I would focus on what was wrong rather than what was right. My expectations were high and my gratitude was low. Thankfully, the Conqueress finally took charge and challenged my skewed perceptions.

For example, there was a gentleman named Ted who I had been dating for a while. We had met just prior to him having to relocate to a neighboring city for a new job opportunity. He would often come stay with me for the weekend. As a result, Ted and his son spent a lot of family-type time with my daughter and me. There was delight in her eyes at the idea of a blended family.

I appreciated all the kind things he had done. There were

handwritten poems on my nightstand. He helped me with home repairs. He was loyal, witty, and attentive. And yet, I couldn't bring those qualities into focus with my shattered lens; all I could see was what was lacking and missing. I spent some time doing inner work, looking at my own self-judgements, and saw that I was projecting those fears and insecurities onto him. With this new viewpoint and outlook, I was able to revive the relationship with even more passion, appreciation, and awareness.

Nevertheless, I still didn't see the relationship progressing the way I had when we first met. Nothing was wrong; it just wasn't right. The combination of the holiday season and my daughter's eagerness to spend time with them, along with her constant questions about marriage, kept my feelings muted longer than they should have. In that discomfort, I was very mindful of my internal signals and subtle knowings of what I needed to do. I loathe hurting people, and this was going to be hard; he really is a great guy. Even more, I worried that I would be perceived as a failure...or worried that I tarnished my daughter by introducing them and allowing the relationship to evolve. I remember thinking to myself, "What have I done?"

The emotions that came up for me were rooted in fear: fear of failure or making a mistake, of hurting others, of judging others, of being alone. At the same time, my awareness of those fears assured me that the thoughts triggering those emotions were not aligned with what I sought in a healthy relationship – healthy for me. It would be a disservice to all involved for me to continue hanging on to something that had reached its expiration date. I recognized that much of the distortion of what a relationship should and shouldn't be came from traditional societal guidelines for what constitutes "a good relationship" and not my own guidelines.

When I noticed those fears rising in my gut, I calmed and reassured myself with my mantra, "I can trust myself." In addition, I recognized that I was staying in the relationship to protect my daughter from having to feel sadness and disappointment.

Wait. That's what I used to do!

I wanted something different for her. I wanted her to have the capacity to feel the full range of her emotions, not to go numb or hide. I wanted her to be emotionally safe, to know that sad things happen and, in time, that she will feel happy again. I need to help her co-regulate her emotions as a child so she'd have the skills as an adult.

I was also inadvertently keeping her fairy-tale illusion alive. That's what I had done my entire childhood and much of my adult life: attach myself to an illusion – a picture of what I thought life would be. I was devastated when my story didn't go as planned. I wanted to do differently for her. I wanted her to know life isn't always as we envision it, and that's okay. I want her to trust something greater than herself. I want her own Conqueress to thrive.

I also noticed how I was continuing that old pattern of making my decisions based on other's feelings while neglecting my own. I worried he would be hurt. I worried my daughter would be disappointed and miss him and his son. I worried my ex-husband would be judgmental. I worried that the outside world would have an opinion on my relationship status. Those were all *external* worries. The Conqueress places a priority on what *she* wants and needs, so I shifted my focus inward.

Having been divorced for eight years at this point, I knew I would be okay. I had rebuilt myself; I was stronger and self-sufficient. It is empowering to be in a place of choosing a partnership out of want rather than need. I had finally learned to be comfortable in my own skin and enjoy time alone. I have hobbies and social activities. I would miss the intimacy and companionship, but all would be well.

Now that the breakup is in my past, I realize that I was mostly afraid of crushing my daughter's dream. In her sweet and child-like way, she frequently imagined a romantic proposal, an exotic destination wedding, family and connection. She was creating a romantic fairy tale story in which I was the main character, the princess in a gown. I could see her wheels turning and how she was counting down the days until our one-year anniversary. Slowly, I began to see that her excitement wasn't really about her; it was about me. More than anything, she wanted to see her mother happy, and staying wasn't making me happy. In fact, staying might prevent her own dream from ever coming true.

"Mom," she said, "If you don't marry, I still want to have a wedding for you."

"Why?" I asked, perplexed.

"I want you to feel special." She smiled.

Too often, we stay in relationships or end them based on what we think the kids want, when in reality they just want us to feel special and be happy.

With this final awareness, I had full confidence in my ability to shift and take action. I didn't know what I wanted, but I knew I needed space to gain clarity and perspective about the relationship. When I took my action step, I confidently answered my initial question of, "What have I done?" In that process, I taught my daughter the following:

1. When something isn't working anymore, it's okay to leave.
2. Always put your needs first; it is also your job to make them known.
3. You can have your heart broken and love again.
4. Each experience brings more clarity to what you want and don't want in life.
5. No regrets. Each person that enters our life has a purpose.
6. Not all things are forever, and that's okay.
7. It takes a long time to know whether you want to spend your life with someone. Keep an open mind and explore your options.
8. When you are true to you, life will turn out better than your wildest expectations.

Through that breakup, what I had been mostly afraid of wasn't even accurate. My daughter wanted me to be happy and staying wasn't the answer. We both had some sadness. She watched me grieve and shed my tears, then watched me move on with freedom and peace and ease. I was happy and so was she.

At this point in my journey, her Dad and I had grown and developed a positive relationship. We had both matured. Essentially, the love we have for our daughter kept propelling us to do the next right thing. When I shared my breakup story with him, he was kind and supportive and offered words of encouragement. He had become my family and friend again. I was so relieved and thankful.

As for what the rest of the world thinks about me or my relationship status, it's irrelevant. It's none of my business to know what they think. What matters is what I think of me. All the fears that were keeping me from moving forward weren't even real. When the Conqueress gives you the nudge, it's time to be courageous, it's time to take action, even if it makes you uncomfortable. In fact, that's the best kind of action.

Acceptance Tool #3: Stay in Gratitude

Feelings of inadequacy can arise, especially when you take a step back and observe the tendency of modern society's constant search for something bigger and better with a never satisfied attitude. The old adage is still wise wisdom – the more 'things' you have, rarely leads to true happiness. It's a textbook effect called hedonic adaptation. With repeated exposure to the same emotion-producing stimulus, we tend to experience less of that emotion. As a result, we become accustomed to the good and desirable life events that happen. Similarly, we also get used to the things we perceive as negative. Said differently, our levels of happiness – or unhappiness – tend to stay the same no matter how much we have.

Hedonic adaptation can generate resiliency and keep us motivated to achieve even greater things, but it also can destroy relationships, ruin jobs, and cause unending purchasing of material possessions if we aren't cautious. When we get used to the people and things that are working well in our lives, we can start taking them for granted, seeing less of the positive and becoming more hyper-focused on the imperfections. It's psychologically imperative to fight hedonic adaptation if we want to maximize happiness.

The way to combat hedonic adaptation is a strong practice of gratitude. It's one of the Conqueress's most powerful tools. The benefits of gratitude are well-documented in science, psychology, and spirituality. In numerous studies, high levels of gratitude have been consistently correlated with more energy and vitality. Gratitude has also been shown to increase self-esteem and reduce insecurity, which means that it can help us focus and improve our productivity.

Spiritual practices invite us to be thankful for what we have and trust that we have all that we need. Keep in mind that gratitude is not a cure-all but a tool for improving life-satisfaction and happiness. It's important to acknowledge that being in gratitude may not always mean that we will never feel angry, mad, or sad. It's important to acknowledge that, because this life is sure to give us the full spectrum of emotions. Recall from our learning in Layer 1, our ability to Feel all of our feelings is critical to our wellbeing and to aligning ourselves with our soul's desires. It is often in experiencing the undesirable emotions that we become aware of the contrast with desirable ones. Knowing the difference, we become forever more grateful for the blessings and benefits of the latter.

As the tangible benefits of gratitude have become validated by science, the tools for incorporating gratitude into our lives have increased exponentially. For example, many of you may have heard of or even used gratitude lists or journals. Gratitude lists are a popular and effective contribution from the field of "positive psychology." The goal of writing what we are grateful for increases our focus on positive experiences – those which ultimately improve well-being. Other gratitude resources, many of them available on the internet, abound. One of my favorites are gratitude meditations. These are a double whammy for well-being because you are essentially performing two of the most impactful happiness practices at the same time.

If you're having a difficult time connecting with feelings of gratitude, ask God, the Universe, a Higher Power, and/or the Conqueress within to help you see the blessings in your life. It can be as simple as the sunshine or a hot cup of coffee. Just start somewhere. I remember having a really hard time finding gratitude after having to abandon my fully furnished, four-thousand-square-foot home with a pool, swim-up bar, and housekeeper and move into a two-bedroom apartment with only a bare minimum of belongings. I meditated on the adage,

"You have to want what you have before you can have what you want."

I began to appreciate and take care of my belongings and that apartment. I became thankful that I only had a small space to keep clean and that I had so many neighbors. I made my bed every morning and made sure my kitchen island sparkled before I went to sleep. I decorated my daughter's room and made sure there were pictures and mementos throughout the house. Suddenly, I enjoyed spending time there! It was as if I needed to show the universe that I would take care of all that I am given, and that if given more, I will continue to be grateful – that I can be trusted to appreciate and care for all that I am blessed with. In time, that apartment led to an even better apartment in the city and eventually to buying a spacious home of my own in an area I loved. I continue to have gratitude by 'wanting what I have so I can have what I want'. Abundance is available to us when we stay open and grateful.

Gratitude journals are a great way to maximize your time and generate feelings of bliss and joy. When you finish meditating on all the blessings, both big and small, I suggest taking time to write them down. Additionally, make a side note as to why you are grateful; this will serve as a powerful reminder in times of challenge when you are feeling less than grateful. It will also capture memories of the positive times. Years ago, I started a family gratitude journal that we keep in our family room. While we are still working on using it regularly, it has been heart-warming to re-experience the precious memories and the little things that have made a big impact on our lives.

When we focus on the positive, stay in gratitude, and use affirming statements, we activate the reward centers of the brain which causes the release of dopamine, releasing feelings of pleasure. These practices create a similar effect to getting a hug or having a hot fudge sundae. I like to think of affirmations as warm, sweet, gooey goodness for our souls. When you repeat the behavior and experience a positive sensation, the more likely you are to keep repeating it. Eventually, these positive tools then become a replacement for the negative, self-defeating patterns and behaviors that no longer serve you.

Acceptance Tool #4: Thank You, I Trust You

After The Fall, when I found myself ruminating and my monkey mind active, I kept going back to my mantra: "Thank you. I trust you." Looking back at my life, I am grateful that so many things *didn't* go the way I wanted them to at that time. Thank God, I didn't get that job. Thank God, that relationship didn't work out. Thank God, I didn't go on that trip. Not experiencing many of the things I thought I wanted — and felt deep sorrow and pain for when they didn't happen — turned out to be a blessing.

Something greater than me knew what was best. This is where my faith and sense of connection to God and the universe didn't require science or proof. My experiences and these feelings of trust and peace and bliss from within were — and are — more valuable and profound than any research article I could read. It's the gentle nudge that I know is guiding me in the right direction. Even when it doesn't seem logical or sane, I thank and I trust in an inner wisdom that knows my heart even better than I know it myself. Coming from someone who has always believed she knows what's best or right, who has navigated through some traumatic and difficult times, who has a hard time trusting others, who has been emotionally abandoned, who has been very guarded to protect herself from pain or disappointment – someone who wants to hold tightly to the reins – it was daunting to let go. But I had no choice. And when I did, a great weight was lifted from my shoulders. I could stand up straight. I could breathe. I didn't have to carry the burdens, the responsibility, and the pain. I could trust. I could be thankful.

The sooner I started accepting that, the sooner I felt peace. It is a peace that I didn't want to lose despite the engrained patterns, old fears, and the illusion of control that keep me trying to force solutions. I would revert back to my mantra: "Thank you, I trust you." The peace comes. Situations unfold far better than I could have ever imagined. So, I trust. I am thankful. In all circumstances. "Thank you. I trust You."

This trust was often put to the test. For example, my ex-husband and I had struggled for three years of court battles and spent what could have been my daughter's college tuition worth of court fees. He had been doing all the things he needed to do for his well-being and to be a healthy Father. There was a flow to our situation, one that was working for everyone, or so I thought. My world froze when he filed for more parenting time. My heart sunk. Fear consumed me. I stopped breathing. At the time, our daughter was only with him 3 hours each week, so I could be confident that all the other hours she would be safe and with me. I didn't want to let her go. I was depleted from the court processes. I was tired of borrowing money and having to ask my parents for help. I fought so hard and so long. This momma bear had claws, the kind that impulsively swipe and protect at all costs.

Although he was taking the appropriate actions and his mental health was stable, I was afraid of his relapse, afraid of what could happen and repeating the turmoil we had just overcome. In all that time, we had not spoken outside the courtroom. Yet, in this particular instant, I meditated on what I should do. I decided to be bold. I picked up the phone. He answered. It was the first time we had talked in all this time. I told him that I had received his request and it would be ok to expand his hours on a trial basis. I said that he could start by having an overnight with our daughter and to see how it went. The conversation was very cordial and brought me great hope, but the walls were still up and claws still intact. We tried the plan, and it was working well. I was glad but felt sheepish for my resistance. After a few months, we agreed to continue and that he would remove his recent court petition to prevent yet another trial and the financial, emotional, and physical stressors that accompanied it. I was elated.

Then, twelve hours before the petition was to be removed, I found out that he had moved one mile from me and wanted 50/50 custody. I was hysterical and panic stricken. I wanted to crumble to the ground. I told him that just because he was physically closer, it didn't make him emotionally, psychologically, or financially ready for this. Trust was still being established. Going back on his word made me question his credibility.

I appeared strong and confident on the outside yet was completely devastated on the inside, feeling hopeless and defeated. I was so tired of the courts, of the never-ending fighting. My mind built up hope that we were moving forward; I took all my action steps and it was time to turn my trust over to something more powerful than me. I surrendered not to him, but surrendered my need for control and yielded, asking for help from my Conqueress.

"Thank you, I trust you," I whispered to God as the tears steadily fell. Each time I wanted to lash out and wonder, "Why me?," I would say, "Thank you, I trust You," fully believing that life was happening for me, not to me. Always a gift, always a blessing. And sometimes in disguise.

Once we were back in court, the judge assigned us to a mediator. We'd been down this road before. Each time we'd pay an excessive amount of money with no resolution. But this time was different. The dreaded scene: the court-appointed therapist, me, and him. She took turns asking me questions and then asking him. I said what I needed to feel comfortable, to move forward. My boundaries were clear. I acknowledged my role and took ownership of the past. The tension in the room dropped and the tightness in his broad shoulders softened. He looked at me with compassion. He told me what I needed to hear. Tears flooded my eyes. With his words of honesty and humility, his heart and radiant soul became visible again. We walked out of the courthouse together and hugged, and laughed, and cried. This was the start of rebuilding our trust and ability to be loving and respectful co-parents.

Looking back, I see the plan did indeed unfold. Had we not gone to court, we probably wouldn't have been forced to collaborate on a solution which led to our healing – a healing that did not just benefit our daughter's life but ours as well. "Thank you, I trust you."

That experience also gave me insight into how much and how hard I will fight for my daughter. What if I started doing the same for myself?

Acceptance Tool #5: Trust that Life Is Happening *for* You

If you look back at your life, I bet you can recall challenging situations that were for your benefit but certainly didn't feel that way at the time. For example, my client Carrie shared how she was really angry that she didn't get accepted into the graduate program she had applied for. As it turned out, the same year as her denial, she landed a job that gave her more exposure to her profession, which later made graduate school much more relevant. Carrie was also diagnosed with a medical condition and hospitalized for much of that year. Had she been attending graduate school, she likely would have had to quit due to her frequent hospitalizations. A year later, her body healed, and she was accepted into the program. She also qualified for a paid internship as a result of her additional work experience.

In another example, my client Amy was devastated when her mentor resigned from her supervising position. The two of them had become very close, and Amy worried how she would manage her job without her close guidance. As it turned out, the two became closer once they stopped working together. Being more independent also allowed Amy to expand her creative visions and exceed her job expectations. She developed more trust and confidence in her own abilities (instead of under the shadows of her boss) and eventually ended up starting her own company, giving her work-life balance and the ability to select only the projects that align with her visions.

Recall the times in your life when you can now see the greater good in a situation. Think back to the times that you were filled with anger, frustration, and despair, trying to will and wish a situation to be different. Filled with "should haves," "would haves," and "could haves." Now fast forward to the present. Do you see how, despite the pain and anguish, what actually happened set you on a better path, taught you a lesson, or opened another door of opportunity? It's helpful to journal on these topics and use them as a point of reference in times when you are feeling that same frustration or disappointment. Over time, you will begin to experience a shift. This shift will allow you to place your trust in something more powerful, more knowing, and more loving than you ever thought possible. You may notice a huge weight being lifted and a sense of joy filling your spirit.

The Layer of Acceptance allowed me to accept life on life's terms. As a result, much of the time I spent consumed with trying to manipulate or control my destiny was now freed. I found myself having fun again and developing new hobbies and interests. The Conqueress was inspired to be creative and delighted in art projects, dance, travel, and yoga. More importantly, the intense need to manage myself and others was gone. A huge burden was finally lifted; I felt lighter and free. I was ready to Transform.

Layer 4: Transform

Imagine. Redefine. Become.

The Conqueress could see and feel her ambitions, her future, and her purpose. She carried them in her dreams and heart. The images of her story were created with her mind in a manner that brought her joy. Through her visualizations, all of her dreams, her visions, and her purposes came into fruition. With ease and grace.

*   *   *

Although we tend to resist or avoid challenges and barriers, we learn to overcome them by identifying and understanding them. The challenges that stand in the way of aligning with our soul's desires can actually assist us in achieving what we desire. These "ah-ha" moments provide understanding that our obstacles to growth are often internal. Examples include insecurity, self-doubt, or feelings of unworthiness; these internal barriers often lead to external barriers. For example, low self-worth may lead to staying in an unhealthy relationship due to false beliefs that you don't deserve better or that no one else would love you. Your external desire may be for a loving and supportive companionship, but you prevent that from happening due to an internal deficit. In order to transform, we have to dig deep to find the true source of the issues that hold us back. Often, for example, the unhealthy relationship is the symptom, not the root cause. To get rid of the symptom, you need to address the problem (e.g., the low self-worth). If you continue to view the person or the relationship as the problem, you can certainly leave that relationship, but your next relationship will likely repeat the same pattern.

Visualization

Transformation starts with visualizing yourself being aligned with what you desire. Think about your desire and how you wish to make it a reality. How do you want to show up in this world, for yourself and others? At this point, you are transforming your narrative – the story of who you are – and your thought patterns to bring about that change. As you start living your life more authentically, you will face obstacles and unfamiliar situations. It's essential to utilize imagery to get past the obstacles. Recall the importance of imagery in both changing brain patterns and activating the vagus nerve. Remember from 'Brain Retrain', how you used affirmations and positive thoughts to break old patterns and create new ones.

Basic Visualization Steps

1. Set aside time free of distractions.
2. Utilize breathwork or meditation to calm the nervous system.
3. Close your eyes and imagine your desired outcome in detail.
4. Be mindful of all of the emotions and sensations this elicits.
5. Practice with consistency.

In general, imagery techniques rely on the use of ideas and visualization rather than logical and deliberate thinking; transforming our life requires that we release over-analyzing, manipulating, and control. To achieve this, we must be deliberate and set aside uninterrupted time and space for creative thinking, exploring, and imagining. For me, this meant setting my alarm earlier and rising before anyone else in the house. As a single parent with full custody of my little girl, though, I know that the time reservation isn't fool proof. If you are struggling to find time, remember that while it's beneficial to establish a routine at the same time each day, it's not required.

At a spiritual level, I began by honoring the time I made for myself as a gift, both asking for and thanking God/the universe for having it. The more I made this simple gesture, the more often time was provided. It was truly amazing. People who knew me would marvel at how much I could fit on my plate. I still begin and end the use of *my* time, whether for mediation, visualization, or exercise, with a "Thank you for this gift of time."

It's also important to start your imagery sessions in a state of calm and comfort. Remember: the quickest way to calm the nervous system is by taking long, slow breaths through the nose. From there, establish the time as your own; everything else has to wait. Clear your mind and create a space to imagine. In doing so, you are using the tools of the Feel layer – breath work, mindfulness, and meditation – to create a pause between stimulus and response. With this sense of clarity and awareness, you will be better equipped to identify and Explore your unwanted belief systems, and practice Acceptance, helping to prepare you to Transform.

Transform Tool #1: DIVA

You may be familiar with the "law of attraction" or other concepts of manifestation which claim that thoughts can change a person's life and that simply having an inspired thought will attract your desires.

It suggests that whether a thought pattern is positive or negative, it will bring that experience into one's life like a self-fulfilling prophecy. Scientifically speaking, the law of attraction has not been validated, yet we do know that our words and thoughts have substantial power. While a single thought (or even a few) won't have the power to manifest, visualizing yourself overcoming obstacles that stand in the way of you and your heart's desire will have a lasting effect.

One of the tools I use with my clients is my DIVA tool: Dream, Identify the Challenge, Visualize Success, Action Steps. To begin this process of transformation, first imagine your "Conqueress dream": What you want and what embodies who you are. In these early stages, it is perfectly acceptable to be a bit of a "diva" – someone who puts herself first and keeps her standards high, who doesn't settle. Spend some time daydreaming and imagining. Explore your innermost desires and what brings you bliss. What would you do and who would you be if there were no limitations? This is a great topic to journal or to create a vision board around. From there, take an honest look at what is standing in your way. Identify the internal challenges or hindrances that prevent you from achieving those dreams. Then, use visualization and imagery to "see" yourself overcoming those challenges and achieving those dreams. In a tool as simple as visualization, there is profound power and impact. You will "see yourself" and "feel" yourself getting what you want in life. With peace. With ease. With joy. With a deep sense of worthiness and deserving and aligning with your soul's purpose.

The DIVA tool has four steps:

1. Dream

Identify your Conqueress dream. This is your truth, your intention, your pleasure. It is not based on the standards that society or others establish for you. For this step, identify and write down that dream. What is your purpose and your passion? What is your heart's desire? What empowers you? To start, choose a goal that feels challenging but is realistic and attainable. It may be helpful to write down what you wish to manifest. For example:

- I want to lose weight.
- I want to learn a new skill.
- I want to be the best parent to our children as possible.
- I want to feel confident and proud of my work.
- I want to improve my physical health.
- I want to learn guitar.
- I want to complete my degree.
- I want to have a happy and healthy marriage.
- I want a job that is fun.
- I want to tap into my spirituality.

Make your own list and just pick one at a time. What is most important to you? You can also ask yourself, "Why do I have this particular dream?" What does the dream mean to you? How will manifesting it change your life? As you reflect on your desire, imagine it as fully as you can. What does it look like? What does it feel like? At this point, you will hopefully have a smile on your face! During this process, be sure to stay in stillness or quiet meditation so you can fully absorb the sensations.

2. Identify the Challenge

What internal obstacles or beliefs are preventing you from achieving this dream? Similar to the Layer 2's Brain Retrain tool, the focus is on your beliefs, emotions, and habits. Time to dig deep. What is it *within* you that holds you back from fulfilling your deepest and highest desires? Get curious and feel that internal challenge. Take a moment to sit in it, stay in that feeling, and experience it fully.

Influences *outside* of you may also present a challenge to your dreams. Obstacles can often be out of our control – mistakenly thinking we can change it leads to frustration and disappointment. In addition, some of these external challenges have underlying internal obstacles. Financial resources, for example, is often a challenge that would be perceived as external. Yet by looking closely at your situation, you may find a connection with lingering internal challenges as well. For example, a fear of failure may be preventing you from applying for a better paying job. Ignorance, fear, or avoidance might be stopping you from learning budgeting and financial planning skills. Has your ego or pride prevented you from asking for help?

All of these stem from previous patterns and beliefs that you are now confronting and transforming as you create new perceptions and narratives. Spend as much time as you need to explore these challenges. Journal, meditate, research, and discuss. Talk to trusted members of your support system; they may have insights you hadn't considered. Acknowledging the challenges and exploring solutions are powerful steps in taking ownership for transforming your life. The alternative is denial and living a life of smallness. By never facing our challenges, we will never feel the full power of the Conqueress.

Train yourself with positive programming, using the tools. Allow the challenges to take shape in your mind's eye. Ask yourself, "What can I do to overcome this challenge?". Write down at least one action you can take or one pinpointed mantra. Recall in Layer 2, the woman who was paralyzed by her fear of public speaking. One of her action steps was to make the time to meditate and use affirmations both prior to and after a presentation. She also sought support. She set boundaries. She activated the Conqueress within and did the uncomfortable things she needed to do in order to overcome her fear and manifest her dream.

Using "if, then" statements can be very beneficial when working with the Transform Layer and seeking behavior change. The statements go something like this:

- "If... (challenge), then I will ... (action or thought)."
- "If I begin to feel performance anxiety, I will take deep breaths and use my affirmations."

3. Visualize Success

Use imagery tools to 'see' yourself overcoming your challenges. As you identify your dream and the challenges that stand in the way of achieving it, take a moment to imagine success as fully as you can either using the following script or allowing yourself to visualize with relaxing music.

Allow your inner desire,
the Conqueress desire,
to come into the mind's eye.
Breathe in and breathe out.
Allow yourself to see it fully and completely.
Notice how it feels.
Allow it to encompass you.
Notice the confidence, the peace, the purpose that accompanies it.
Continue to allow it to exude you,
Every part, every fiber, of your being.
Breathing in and breathing out.
Breathing in and breathing out.
Now see yourself using your tools,
your strategies,
your mantras
To overcome your obstacles
with ease, with purpose, with grace.
A smile comes across your face.
Let go of any discomfort as you embrace the sensations that arise.
As you visualize this conquering, notice
how quickly the barriers dissipate.
You align with your desire, the Conqueress desire.
It is pure. It is true. It is You.
Allow yourself to be immersed in this.
Feel proud.
Feel accomplished.

Know you are worthy.
You are the Conqueress.

*   *   *

Let this experience marinate as long as you can,
Reminding yourself that this peace, this confidence, this security,
this manifestation is always available to you.

4. Action Steps

Achieving your dream is within your grasp when you begin to take action steps. It's no longer just a dream; it is an experience that is now available to you. By allowing the dream to expand beyond your imagination, and instead into action steps, you are on your way to achieving your vision. Use your actions to overcome the challenge. Spend time in visualization. See yourself feeling empowered: confident, happy, and complete in your new role. Feel it in your mind, body, and soul. If doubts arise, push them away. Know the dream is yours and will be done.

Transform Tool #2: Re-tell Your Story

The use of imagery proved to be greatly effective in my healing journey. As I continued my exploration, I became aware of just how much I yearned for attention and affection from both of my parents as a child. It was especially hard for me, because while they were physically present, the overwhelming reality of having five children in six years, along with all the financial and familial struggles that go with it, left little time to devote to me.

I knew that my parents were genuine and good people. Like all of us, their own conditioning, beliefs, and life struggles left them incapable of meeting my needs in a way that I needed them to be met. Their own life experiences may have prevented them from aligning with their true selves. They grew up during a time of rapid technological advances and a powerful shift in focus from basic survival needs to tending to psychological well-being. Perhaps they hadn't been taught or shown how to give and receive love and affection, develop appropriate communication skills, or how to set boundaries. Whether or not love was expressed in the manner I wanted and needed, I still knew that the love and desire existed within them.

In my visualization, I recreated my story in a space without hardships or conditioning – only love and peace. I saw myself as three years old with long pigtails and a yellow-flowered romper that I remember seeing myself wear in numerous family photos. I was at the beach. The sun was gleaming, and the waves made a soft rush against the shore. My parents were there; I knew them by their energy, their aura.

The man, my Dad, was tall and lean with sun-kissed hair, a gentle smile, and a hearty laugh. He didn't carry the emotional and physical weight he does in reality, nor was his face red and stressed. He had a peace I had never felt or known him to have. It made me sad to know how much burden and stress he had to carry for his whole life. I also gained an awareness that his inability to nurture me in my early years wasn't personal. He did love me; he just didn't know how to show it. He had never been taught.

My Mom was hippie-looking with her golden, blonde hair and flowered, flowy dress, her feet bare and pristine. She exuded a peace and harmony that was magnetic. Her aura was of complete and pure love, free of the financial, emotional, and physical stresses of raising five kids and managing a busy household. Unweighted by judgment and the ridicule of others. In her highest and best self, undamaged by the conditioning and patterning of her own life, she yearned to love me the way I needed to be loved.

As a young girl, I remember desperately trying to grasp any attention I could. I remember choosing German Chocolate Cake for my birthday each year, not because I liked it, but because it was my Dad's favorite. I endured years of band class playing the clarinet to appease my Mom. I would diligently try to get good grades and over-achieve. Looking back, I wish I'd had the skills and ability to articulate my feelings and ask for what I needed. But I didn't, and as a result, my body, mind, and soul have suffered.

In my visualization, I wanted to tell them that I needed their love and affection, but I didn't need to in that visionary place. Now that I could see and feel their true auras, the past was irrelevant. This brought me so much peace. We sat on that beach for hours. They held me tightly and showered me with words of affection as the waves crashed against the coastline and the sun beamed upon us. Their love encompassed me in a way I had never experienced. It was unconditional. In all of my childhood, there was never a moment of just me and my parents. There was never enough time nor space in a big family like mine.

I felt empathy as I compared the quantity of time that I get to solely focus on my daughter, something my parents were never granted. I realized how they might have missed out on deep quality time with their children. More than likely, they wanted to be different, and maybe they wished steps were more intentional instead of just surviving the chaos. In an odd way, this also brought me peace. I realized the pain of my childhood wasn't because I was unlovable or unworthy; it simply wasn't within their capacity. Today, I carry their love with me. I bring myself to those visualizations at the beach and connect with the abundance of love, guidance, and support. I now know. I have always been lovable and worthy, simply by being me.

Similar to my vision, it's within your capacity to re-create or re-tell your own story. Think back to a time, a place, or situation that still causes emotional pain. Allow yourself to feel empathy for the trouble others have endured; it was their own way of coping. However it may have harmed you, it was the best they knew how to do.

Understandable Can Still Be Unacceptable

It's important to remember that understandable does not always equate to acceptable. Knowing why a person "is the way they are" does not make it okay for them to treat you badly. You can feel compassion for their own pain, but that doesn't mean their hurtful actions correlate with your self-worth. In fact, most people's actions and behaviors are a direct result of their relationship with themselves. When we let go of the old stories that improperly steered us otherwise, we can recreate healthier outcomes.

Memories are only perceptions of a situation – how our brain encodes our feelings and interpretations. You may not have liked the outfit you wore or how your mom curled your hair, but your mom's recollection of the same event may have been delight because she thought your hair was beautiful and trendy. Different people can also have different memories of the same experience. For example, a conversation at work can lead one person to recall it with exhilaration and another to feel disappointment. None of it is the ultimate truth; they are all just perceptions based on our experiences. Since this is so, we have the capability to re-create and re-tell a story to align with our needs.

Give yourself space and time to fully utilize this tool. Re-imagine a particular scenario or take yourself to a completely different place with the same people. Take notice of the details. What do you see? What do you hear? What do you feel? Notice yourself feeling grounded and connected to the earth – at peace.

Allow the person or people involved to come into your mind. See them through a heartful and forgiving lens. Take the opportunity to see the very best version of them – perhaps a version they have yet to even see themselves. Fill that image with love, peace, and healing. When you have released any negative emotions, allow your mind to re-imagine the energy of the original experience to align with your needs. Hold on to those sensations and store them in your memory so they can be easily retrieved. Every time you bring them up, see them through lens of love. In this process, you will also notice a shift in compassion toward yourself.

Transform Tool #3: Detach with Love

Many families struggle with *enmeshment*: being overly involved in every aspect of one another's lives to the point that it prohibits them from establishing an independent sense of self. It's the root of codependent behavior which is often carried into romantic partnerships. When a certain behavior is a baseline for 'normal', it becomes familiar and comfortable, making it very difficult to gravitate toward something different. Make no mistake: "familiar plus comfortable" does not always equal healthy.

I've learned some profound lessons in co-dependency. I was always the caretaker, concerned about the wellbeing of others ahead of my own needs. In so doing, I later learned that I was enabling others, no matter their behavior. By allowing and accepting those unhealthy behaviors and actions, I denied them not only the opportunity to be successful but also to fail. Therefore, I was ultimately denying them of their own way of healing. When I first heard the term "detach with love," I completely struggled with the idea. My over-involved mind wanted to keep believing I had all the answers, and that I could make the situation right, make it better.

Most of the people we have co-dependent relationships with, we do love, or at least like them. It may be either an obligatory or an unconditional love driven by bloodlines or past traumas and life experiences. It may be a sibling, someone that you'll always love, yet your interactions are toxic. Or maybe it's with a child who is struggling with addiction and is always stealing from you and blaming you. These are hard and painful experiences. The heart wants to believe in the good in others, yet we must protect ourselves and stay balanced on that three-legged stool (mind, body, soul). We must train our minds to detach with love.

One of the most profound tools I used to get through some of my darkest moments was detaching with love visualizations. This imagery tool is a simple yet effective way to protect us from taking on the energy, responsibilities, and harm that do not belong to us. This tool can be used in conjunction with setting healthy boundaries and parameters but not as a replacement for them. To be clear, these tools are for *emotional* protection. If there is abuse or neglect, more intensive support and intervention may be needed.

This technique involves visualizing a radiant, white healing light surrounding the person or object that is interfering with our wellbeing. As you surround them with this supportive light, visualize yourself gently pushing them away. If you choose to, you may also invite a Higher Power to accompany them on their journey. It's a beautiful way to detach with love. Love isn't black or white. It is possible to love someone while deterring a relationship you know won't work. It is possible to wish someone well and not take ownership for helping them. It is possible for a behavior to be both understandable and unacceptable. All too often, our thinking is black and white. The truth is, most things are complex and somewhere between black and white. Until we see the range of options that exist between black and white, we limit ourselves and continue cycles of dysfunction.

I still vividly recall thinking that I knew what my ex-husband needed and how to help him. I decided that prior to actually seeing him, I would start imagining him. I would visualize a healing white light around him. I would wish him health and wellness and prosperity. I would acknowledge that it wasn't my job or even within my ability to know what was best for him. I would also imagine a healing white light around me. This was my aura of protection, my shield of security. Then I would lovingly push him and his white bubble of light away. I would take a few deep breaths and repeat an affirmation: "Bless him and bless me. God's will be done. May we both be free from suffering." Peace would replace the fear. Then miraculously, when I did come face-to-face with him, the tension between us seemed to become diffused a little bit more every time.

Detaching from Outcomes

Not only does the Conqueress detach from the negative emotional energy of others, but she detaches from outcomes. All too often, our false outcomes are what society has defined as the prerequisites for happiness. In all the conditioning and patterning of our life prior to this moment, standards of success have been glorified and magnified. We may think that happiness comes in the form of a specific career path, the perfect spouse, two kids and a dog, the white picket fence, and the fancy car. How often does that hold true? Maybe on the Hallmark channel, Netflix episode, or Facebook posts, but those outlets only show momentary bouts of happiness rather than the full spectrum of challenges and obstacles, the hurt and pain. Illusions of happiness are just that – illusions. They are not guaranteed models of success. There is no one size fits all. We are each unique individuals with unique talents, desires, and purpose.

If we choose to adhere to what others define as success, we will stay small and dissatisfied. The Conqueress will remain buried but continue to cry out to be known. You will never experience the deep contentment of aligning with your soul's purpose. Nothing has brought me more joy than being of service, sharing my stories and knowledge, and facilitating healing in others. It is my definition of success, my reason for being here, my purpose. When I'm aligned with that, my life flows in every area: family, security, and work. Stress and worry are an afterthought.

It's perfectly acceptable to desire financial freedom, the ability to travel, love and companionship. It is perfectly fine to want abundance; it's available to you and you are deserving. You don't have to play the victim role. The tool of transformation is about defining *your* Conqueress version of success rather than what society, your parents, your partner, your children, your peers, or anyone else believes should be success for you. You can certainly listen to their ideas, but in the end, choose what resonates with the Conqueress within and thank the universe for the opportunity to align with your soul's desire and purpose.

As a parent, I understand the nuances of assuming we know what's best for our kids. We truly desire our children to be happy and successful, to live and love beyond their wildest dreams. As parents, we feel responsible for guiding them on their path. Yet it's important to be mindful of the difference between *facilitating* and *forcing*. It's fine to offer suggestions, examples, and ideas. It's also necessary to establish boundaries and consequences. To this day, one of the greatest things I have done with my daughter is to consistently show that my love is unconditional. Her face lights up, her shoulders relax, and I sense her peace when I say, "Sweetheart, I love you all the time. There is nothing you could do that would make me stop loving you. I may not like all of your choices, and I may give you consequences, but my love never changes."

By talking with our children, reminding them that our love is unconditional, and admitting our own mistakes, they will become more adept at developing their own path and aligning with themselves in a way that leads to success. They will learn to listen to their Conqueress intuition and believe in themselves. When we align with our purpose, the result will always be satisfaction and success. Every. Single. Time.

Aligning to our true purpose is a simple yet challenging concept, especially in a society that has emphasized competition and materialism as the means to happiness. Only when you realize it's a convincing myth will you see your path to happiness. Know that it is possible to have both happiness and material comfort, as long as your intentions are properly prioritized.

First, allow yourself to align with your heart's desire. And instead of getting attached to a specific outcome, determine the qualities or sensations you want to experience from a desired outcome. Let's say that you apply for director of marketing at a large firm and are headstrong in your opinion that this is the only job for you. That is likely your ego talking – thinking you know what's best. Then you get the job! Don't be surprised if the initial euphoria you experience are hard to sustain. Is your joy derived from the job itself or the satisfaction of getting the job? If the latter, that novelty and sense of accomplishment will typically wear down, and soon enough you'll be off on your next pursuit of happiness.

Now, let's say you didn't get the job. Imagine the heartache, disappointment, and blow to your self-worth. These outcomes can lead to depression and other negative consequences. Again, ask yourself: Is your disappointment about not getting a job or that *particular* job? So often we get overly attached to an idea of what we want instead of digging deeper to recognize if it's what we actually want.

By detaching from outcomes, we can let go of the illusion of control and place our confidence in something bigger than us, trusting that life is unfolding exactly as it's meant to. Focus on values and inner satisfaction. Stay open to opportunities that best align with your greatest desire.

Let's go back to the job example. Rather than becoming obsessed with a particular outcome or specific position, focus on what you want a job to bring to your life. What will inspire happiness and joy? For some, the ideal job will provide financial stability, flexibility for family, opportunities to shine and be creative, positive team rapport, being of service, and/or a chance to learn and grow. Take some time and "get raw" with the values and sensations you want to feel in that job. Trust that the universe gets the message. When you do, you will open yourself to opportunities and situations you may never have considered otherwise. Then if you don't get a particular job, you can be confident that the universe is telling you it doesn't meet your needs; there is a better one waiting for you.

Another client I worked with was a beautiful and intelligent woman who kept falling into the same relationship patterns. She tended to focus on men who looked a certain way: dark, tall, and handsome. In her mind, she associated that "look" with the perfect mate. And yet one by one, they seemed to disappoint and not meet her expectations. When we started to focus on how she wanted to feel in a relationship, the energy started to shift. She wanted to feel respected and valued. She wanted laughter and to have mutual interests. She wanted physical connection and chemistry. She wanted children and a family. She desired a partner who had financial stability and responsibility. She visualized herself happy and in love. She trusted her Higher Power to find the person that her heart desired. She stayed open to creative possibilities. In a relatively short time, a new man entered her life. At first, she thought he wasn't her "type." But when she paused, she realized that all of her heart's desires were aligned and soon found herself with a ring on her finger. To this day, she attributes her success in finding "the right man" to shifting away from an endless cycle of online dating and "images" of the perfect mate.

Love without Attachments

Not only does the Conqueress detach with love, but she also can discern the difference between Love and Attachment. Many confuse love with what is actually an attachment. If you find yourself grasping and clinging in a relationship because you are afraid to lose love, that is attachment. Love, on the other hand, wants people to be happy – even if it means losing someone in a relationship. Attachment and love cannot co-exist.

Love is beautiful and satisfying. Love is also vulnerable and subjects us to disappointment, heartache, and loss. Losing a relationship means we may have to suffer, and humans are often afraid to suffer and mistakenly cling to attachment as a solution. In reality, the more tightly we hold on to others, the more we suffer. We deprive ourselves of receiving true love because we are consumed with staying attached to something that may not be love. Keeping our guard up because of fear also prevents love from coming in. When we let go and allow both sides of the relationship to be as we are, a space is created to meet together in wholeness and happiness. This is love.

Society paints an inaccurate picture that the more tightly we hold on, the more we show love, and that the more we sacrifice, the more we are loving. Attachment clings to the idea that fulfilment can only be found through another. The reality is that the looser the grip, the greater the chance to be oneself and allow true bonding to occur. I know it sounds counterintuitive, but if two people enter a relationship already fulfilled, whole and without an expectation of happiness, the likelihood of real love goes up. The freedom to have both space and support is key for a lasting, authentic relationship. This is what happened with Gilbert. After taking space from him, I had gained clarity and perspective. I was ready to come back. As I reached out, I did so with some apprehension; I was placing myself in a position in which I could suffer, be criticized, be rejected. But the Conqueress knew what she wanted, so I picked up the phone and called him.

"Hi baby," he said. "I've missed you. How is your heart?" I exhaled into love.

Space had given us the opportunity to fully see one another and accept each other exactly as we were – to excitedly step toward one another. There was no clinging; just a desired nearness which permitted us to come together while being true to our authentic self. This was different for me. It was love. It didn't reflect the attachment scenarios played out over and over on "reality TV," social media, and online dating, which have become the norm. I've watched my fair share of reality shows and my ten-year-old daughter has caught bits and pieces. The confused looks on her face and raised eyebrows speak volumes about how even a child can recognize the absurdities when someone who hasn't even had a conversation with a possible mate and then doesn't "get the rose" breaks down hysterically. This is a modern-day example of attachment versus love. Clearly the individual wants to fall in love, but in some of these cases, the despair may be more about not winning the prize than the loss of love. Still, rejection is painful, and at some level, she may measure her self-worth by her failure to "win." But we aren't born to compete for approval, which is often mistaken for love. This is faulty wiring.

When we don't get attached to outcomes, we interpret the same experiences very differently. The Conqueress views love and potential relationships with the goal of being true to herself. If she isn't selected, it isn't personal. It's not rejection. It was simply a sign that there's something better for her. She would thank the universe for the opportunity and trust that love was somewhere else.

Your Body

The Conqueress honors her body as an expression of love. She is both sexy and modest. The act of intimacy should feel like two souls dancing in harmony. It is the body's way to express love and gratitude.

As you work through the Layers, your relationship with your body will begin to change. In the past, we may have used our bodies to attract mates, manipulate, gain attention, and seek approval. It became the measure of our self-worth. Using the physical body in this way, however, makes us susceptible to rejection, abuse, or neglect. When this happens, we take it personally, believing that we aren't thin enough, curvy enough, or muscular enough. Whatever "the goal," we believe we aren't enough. This is the engrained message for far too many women.

However others see us, our bodies do not define our worth. We are all sexy, beautiful creatures! So, when embracing your sexy actions, fashion, or how you speak, ask yourself, "Am I expressing my love and gratitude or trying to gain approval, attention, and affection? Am I using my sexual nature to manipulate and control or as a means of connection and intimacy?"

When you use the body to create an attachment, you subject yourself to self-judgment and negative perceptions. When you use your body to express love, you will begin to view and treat it with love. When you use your sexuality with the honor, self-respect, and dignity it was intended for, you will begin to accept your body. You will no longer worry about what others think or how you compare. You will begin to delight in the body and your ability to express love without attachment.

Transform Tool #4: Boundary Setting

After peeling through the Layers, I needed to protect myself, my new identity, and the healing work that had been done. The best way to do this by setting healthy boundaries. Boundaries are essentially the way we teach others how we want to be treated – what we'll accept and what we won't. Unfortunately, we aren't born knowing how to do this and usually haven't been taught. Rather, we mimic the same poorly attempted or lack of boundaries that were modeled for us, reflecting generations of ineffective boundary setting. This may include yelling and rage or becoming a doormat – allowing others to trample over your feelings and needs. The lack of appropriate modeling and teaching have left many of us with inadequate coping mechanisms and unhealthy habits which then lead to poor boundary-setting skills.

When it comes to setting boundaries and teaching others how you want to be treated, keep the following in mind:

- Say What You Mean.
- Mean What You Say.
- Don't Say It Mean.
- Know You Aren't Mean.

Say What You Mean.

Boundary setting requires being honest with yourself about what YOU want, not what you think others want for you. Let go of any tendency to people-please. This is about honoring and pleasing yourself. This your Conqueress truth.

Mean What You Say.

When you set a boundary, be sure it's a line you are willing to enforce. If not, you lose credibility. For example, a parent may tell a child that if they continue arguing, they won't be allowed to go on the family vacation. The parent needs to ask themselves, "Are we willing to enforce that?" Or would a consequence such as losing electronic privileges for 24 hours be more reasonable? Avoid ultimatums unless you are committed to carrying them out.

Don't Say It Mean.

The way we relay a message has a huge impact on how others will react. Communicate in a calm yet firm manner. Always make sure your central nervous system is relaxed when setting boundaries. It is crucial to be in your best thinking when taking these brave actions.

Know You Aren't Mean.

Women in particular may feel guilt when setting a boundary. Often, this type of guilt is another example of faulty wiring from your past. If you don't take care of yourself, who will? Keep in mind that if you haven't set boundaries in the past, it may be difficult for those around you to adapt, especially those players in your life who tend to take advantage of you or are not accustomed to you having a voice.

They may get upset or frustrated, and that is okay. I have found that the people who truly want the best for me eventually come to respect and accept my boundaries, whether they agree or not. So model strength and courage, especially for others. Stand up for yourself. Honor your Conqueress.

The Unfolding

$\mathcal{E}$arly in our marriage, I remember hearing a quote: "Every knock is a boost." Although I didn't really comprehend the significance of those words at the time, they stuck with me. As I evolved, I began to realize that every time life knocked me down, I had the chance to get up and use that experience to boost me into a forward motion. Each time I experienced adversity, I could use it to fuel my desire to overcome. Each time I was challenged, I could be resilient and tenacious. Every knock allowed me to grow stronger, bolder, and more confident in my Conqueress self.

As the days and years passed, my ex-husband and I slowly restored the trust and respect that had been bulldozed over during The Fall. Many are quick to say that, "Time heals," when it comes to grief, disappointment, and heartache. I disagree.

Many emotions do heal, but it's not the time that does the healing. Rather, healing is the result of specific changes and actions: a shift in perspective, an apology or forgiveness, a deep grieving. I say this because anger, resentments, judgment, and pride can actually accumulate over time. So, it's not the time that dictates healing; healing is the result of our conscious actions and behaviors during that time. Time is a gift to be used wisely.

All of my knockdowns paved the way for many boosts. The Conqueress ruled as I set boundaries, spoke my truth, agreed to disagree, and kept my integrity. Trust was slowly re-established. I noticed that my ex-husband started to really listen and value my opinions. More importantly, he respected my boundaries, even when he didn't agree. He became honest even when it was hard. We made amends and considered the other's viewpoint. We prioritized our daughter and our roles in her life. We offered grace and compassion to each other.

This healing allowed me to release my resentments and anger. It alleviated my fear of the future. I could be present without being haunted by my past or anxious about what was next. I achieved this FEAT as a result of using my tools to Feel, Explore, Accept, and Transform. I felt my emotions and explored them. I accepted what is and I transformed.

He and I have lived the extremes. We've experienced the complete absence of communication and connection and have confided and supported one another. We have sat as far apart as possible at our daughter's school functions and have walked in to events side-by-side. We have argued over minor things and have shared words of support and encouragement. We have been hateful and shown respect. We know the contrast, and I think that's why we fight so hard to maintain a positive co-parenting relationship. When we do, our daughter wins. We have shown up and fought for her in different ways – ways that are true to who we each are as individuals. While our opinions still vary, it is this fight that propels us to see the other partner as sharing an undying love for our child. That type of love is beyond reproach. I am grateful for the time we spent together in our marriage and accept that our time as husband and wife is over. There is no reason to hate. My love for him is deep. I see his soul and it is good.

Vinn

Elyse, my daughter, had been longing for a puppy for quite some time. So when I was offered a white, three-pound fluffball of love (one that didn't shed!), I couldn't refuse. To this day, he is still Elyse's best friend, and the day she got him is her all-time favorite memory. As I knew it would be a memorable day for her, I invited her Dad to be part of the surprise. I also invited my sisters; it would be the first interaction they had with my ex-husband since The Fall years prior. I reminded myself that I was not responsible for other's behaviors or emotions, nor could I control them. This was meant to be a memorable experience and I decided to be present and joyful. And it turned out to be all of those things!

We agreed to decide on a name together. I tend to focus on the meaning of names; Elyse means "God's promise." I started Googling names associated with joy and came across Vinn, which also meant "to Conquer." Elyse liked it, and so we agreed. At the time, I hadn't even contemplated writing a book, let alone knew what the title would be. God works in subtle ways, yes?

At this point, her Dad and I were cordial but not close. We communicated when we had to, and exclusively on parenting issues. Although Vinn is technically my dog, Elyse wanted Vinn to stay with her whether she was with her Dad or me. Being the animal lover that he is and working from home, her Dad readily agreed.

Having to potty train a puppy is no joke. This would take a team effort, and her Dad's ability to be home with him on his days with Elyse and take him for walks was priceless. Looking back, Vinn the Conqueror became a catalyst for drawing our family together. We became a collaborative force in caring for the newest member of our non-traditional family. He also gave us the opportunity to be humble and support each other. By recognizing the strength that another parent or partner can offer, alliances are enhanced. You realize you're on the same team. You both want what's best. And while you may have different ideas of how to get there, you become open to each other's opinions and ideas and become more willing to find solutions together. Vinn gave us that gift and made it easier to carry those skills into co-parenting our daughter. Vinn, the white fluff ball of "Joy," allowed us to "Conquer" our fears and distrust from the past and move toward a collaborative relationship. I believe it can be said for both our pets and our babies that the undying love they inspire, and our dedication to their wellbeing overpowers the ego and liberates our best selves.

Family

My ex-husband had been a star basketball player. I had always envisioned him teaching and coaching her in sports. When that didn't happen, I was left with having to release my resentment and disappointment. I'm not sure how or why, but when she entered the fifth grade, things changed. Her Dad had installed a new basketball new rim in his driveway, and we enrolled her into a league.

For Elyse's first game, my ex-husband and I agreed to drive together since we would both be attending. This was during the COVID-19 pandemic and the games were held outside. As such, he brought Vinn. When we are all together, Vinn's excitement is through the roof – and contagious. We were all genuinely happy.

He and I sat together, cordial and respectful and, most importantly, genuine. We are friends. We are family. We care for and support each other. We cheered for our daughter and made small talk throughout the game. At half-time, I took a deep breath. Here, in front of me, was the vision I had once grieved was forever lost – a vision of my family at the park, playing and laughing. And while it wasn't the way I thought it would be, in its non-traditional way, it was even better. Family, connection, laughter, unity. We were exactly that. Even though we no longer had a romantic relationship, we could still be family. We still *are* family. And I can still have a romantic relationship outside my non-traditional family which, in time, could also become an extension of that family. Coming to terms with those concepts has taken time, but they have made me a better person.

The biggest moment of clarity came when I realized our relationship didn't have to be black and white. Just because we were divorced (and not "in love") didn't mean we had to hate one another. I cannot hate someone I once loved. It was comforting when I allowed myself to still love him, even in a much different way. That shift aligned with my Conqueress. I knew this to be true because as soon as I accepted it, I had peace.

The Christmas (Non)Miracle

It was Christmas Day; my ex-husband and I sat on the patio and sipped coffee while our daughter stayed inside my house enjoying her gifts. This once stranger in my husband's body was now my family again. We started to reminisce, talking openly about important issues and confiding in each other. As I shared some of my emotions, he compared me to a modern-day warrior goddess: a bloodstained yet strong-willed, politically astute, and courageous woman who recognizes the emotional, physical, and spiritual growth that has come with each new struggle I'd been given.

What I saw in him was a commitment to his family; he exemplified honesty, integrity, vulnerability, and open-mindedness. Perhaps the Conqueror within him had emerged. Perhaps it took hitting rock bottom and remembering the love of our child to awaken our higher angels: to do better, to want more, and be more.

Some may consider this moment between us a Christmas miracle. Again, I would disagree. Given the toxicity at the time of The Fall, our current reconciliation would certainly seem highly improbable. But it didn't occur by chance or divine intervention alone. Had I not worked through my own layers of Feeling, Exploring, Acceptance, and Transformation, I do not believe this reconciliation would have occurred. I do give great credit and honor to the divine wisdom that guided me each step of the way. But the hard work of healing still had to be done by me.

Perhaps

Perhaps The Fall wasn't a fall at all. Perhaps what seemed at the time to be my world crashing down was actually something more powerful than a rerouting of my path. Perhaps my despair was without merit. Perhaps this was always meant to be my journey. Perhaps this all-knowing force knew better. Perhaps this was the only way for my purpose and passion to be fulfilled. And perhaps my testimony will allow you to Trust.

Our Conscious Shift

While we cannot change the past, we can develop a consciousness and a deeper understanding and bring balance to the present. The truth of the matter is that while we can keep up with the many advances of the modern world, we have been going about it in the wrong way. Each shift, each advance, each new horizon has been accompanied by a false panic to keep up. Busyness and immediate gratification have consumed our attention at the expense of our social-emotional wellbeing: we became neglected and regarded as insignificant.

Our world is accelerating at an astonishing rate. Amazing inventions and possibilities seem to happen every day. Now imagine what we could accomplish if we were in true alignment, balanced in mind, body, and soul. As the Conqueress knows, that balance is achieved with stillness. The irony is that in order to "keep up," we must slow down.

As our eyes open each morning, we have a choice. We can choose to engage in the hustle and bustle of the news, social media, and the dramas of the day – even before we've brushed our teeth! In doing so, we over-stimulate the nervous system and trigger our brain into "fight, flight, or freeze" mode. Setting the day in this way tends to lead to stress, anxiety, reactive decision-making and, ultimately overwhelm. It is hard to hear the voice of the Conqueress when consumed with these negative sensations.

We can also choose to slow down – to be still and listen. We can make time to breath, meditate, read inspirational messages, journal, or become mindful of our surroundings. When we make such a conscious choice with acts of self-care and a calm nervous system, we set a very different tone for the day. We prepare ourselves for the day's unfolding from a place of grounded logic and love.

To help counterbalance the noise and distractions of our world, we must first prioritize for ourselves and our needs. This conscious shift in perspective will restore our social-emotional wellbeing. When we are so aligned, the Conqueress governs with an inner wisdom that knows who we were created to be, what brings us passion, when the timing is right, where we will find peace, and how we can manifest our purpose. In this space, the why's don't matter. The workings of the Conqueress are often beyond our comprehension. But when we start building a trust within ourselves and feel the protection of a wise, loving force, we will move forward with great momentum.

The Conqueress Within

You are not here by coincidence or accident. You are meant to be the person you were designed to be. Believe in yourself and do the healing work. Know that life is unfolding exactly as it's meant to so that you gain the experiences you need to evolve and conquer. You are a seeker. Keep taking steps to discover your life purpose and dedicate yourself in a manner that aligns accordingly. Living with empowerment will bring meaning and fulfillment to your life and betterment to those around you. You now have the Tools to transform your life. The outcome will exceed your wildest dreams. The Conqueress knows how to achieve what is truly right for you.

References

Barnett, Jeffrey E. "Are Religion and Spirituality of Relevance in Psychotherapy?" *Spirituality in Clinical Practice* 3, no. 1 (2016): 5–9. https://doi.org/10.1037/scp0000093.

Bayer, Laurence, Irina Constantinescu, Stephen Perrig, Julie Vienne, Pierre-Paul Vidal, Michel Mühlethaler, and Sophie Schwartz. "Rocking Synchronizes Brain Waves during a Short Nap." *Current Biology* 21, no. 12 (June 2011): R461–62. https://doi.org/10.1016/j.cub.2011.05.012.

D'Angelo, James. *The Healing Power of the Human Voice: Mantras, Chants, and Seed Sounds for Health and Harmony.* Vermont: Inner Traditions/Bear & Co, 2005.

Damerla, Venugopal R., Babette Goldstein, David Wolf, Krishna Madhavan, and Nancy Patterson. "Novice Meditators of an Easily Learnable Audible Mantram Sound Self-Induce an Increase in Vagal Tone during Short-Term Practice: A Preliminary Study." *Integrative Medicine: A Clinician's Journal* 17, no. 5 (October 1, 2018): 20–28.

Davis, Daphne M., and Jeffrey A. Hayes. "What Are the Benefits of Mindfulness? A Practice Review of Psychotherapy-Related Research." *Monitor on Psychology* 43, no. 7 (July/August 2012). https://www.apa.org/monitor/2012/07-08/ce-corner.

Detko, Eva. *Mind-Body and the Vagus Nerve Connection Transcripts [Transcripts from Seven Day Training from Various Professionals Regarding the Vagus Nerve]*, 2020. Ebook.

Doidge, Norman. *The Brain That Changes Itself: Stories of Personal Triumph from the Frontiers of Brain Science*. Victoria, Australia: Scribe Publications, 2010.

Grossman, Paul, Ludger Niemann, Stefan Schmidt, and Harald Walach. "Mindfulness-Based Stress Reduction and Health Benefits." *Journal of Psychosomatic Research* 57, no. 1 (July 2004): 35–43. https://doi.org/10.1016/s0022-3999(03)00573-7.

Hazlett-Stevens, Holly, and Michelle G. Craske. "Breathing Retraining and Diaphragmatic Breathing." In *General Principles and Empirically Supported Techniques of Cognitive Behavior Therapy*, edited by William T. O'Donohue and Jane E. Fisher, 166–72. New Jersey: John Wiley & Sons, 2009.

Horowitz, Sala. "Health Benefits of Meditation: What the Newest Research Shows." *Alternative and Complementary Therapies* 16, no. 4 (August 2010): 223–28. https://doi.org/10.1089/act.2010.16402.

Hülsheger, Ute R., Hugo J. E. M. Alberts, Alina Feinholdt, and Jonas W. B. Lang. "Benefits of Mindfulness at Work: The Role of Mindfulness in Emotion Regulation, Emotional Exhaustion, and Job Satisfaction." *Journal of Applied Psychology* 98, no. 2 (2013): 310–25. https://doi.org/10.1037/a0031313.

Jensen, Eric. *Enriching the Brain: How to Maximize Every Learner's Potential*. New Jersey: John Wiley & Sons, 2009.

King, Dana E., and Bruce Bushwick. "Beliefs and Attitudes of Hospital Inpatients about Faith Healing and Prayer." *Journal of Family Practice* 39, no. 4 (October 1994): 349–52.

Longhurst, John C. "Defining Meridians: A Modern Basis of Understanding." *Journal of Acupuncture and Meridian Studies* 3, no. 2 (June 2010): 67–74. https://doi.org/10.1016/s2005-2901(10)60014-3.

Mandalaneni, Kesava, and Appaji Rayi. *Vagus Nerve Stimulator.* Florida: StatPearls Publishing, 2021.

McClelland, Megan M., and Shauna L. Tominey. "The Development of Self-Regulation and Executive Function in Young Children." *Zero to Three* 35, no. 2 (2014): 2–8.

Murray, Desiree W., Katie Rosanbalm, Christina Christopoulos, and Amar Hamoudi. "Self-Regulation and Toxic Stress: Foundations for Understanding Self-Regulation from an Applied Developmental Perspective (OPRE Report #2015-21)." Washington, DC: Office of Planning, Research and Evaluation, Administration for Children and Families, US Department of Health and Human Services, 2015.

Perrault, Aurore A., Abbas Khani, Charles Quairiaux, Konstantinos Kompotis, Paul Franken, Michel Muhlethaler, Sophie Schwartz, and Laurence Bayer. "Whole-Night Continuous Rocking Entrains Spontaneous Neural Oscillations with Benefits for Sleep and Memory." *Current Biology* 29, no. 3 (February 2019): 402–11. https://doi.org/10.1016/j.cub.2018.12.028.

Peter, Levine. "Peter Levine PhD on Trauma: How the Body Releases Trauma and Restores Goodness." Digital Seminar (Live Webcast). *PESI*, May 1, 2018.

Pruett, James M., Nancy J. Nishimura, and Ronnie Priest. "The Role of Meditation in Addiction Recovery." *Counseling and Values* 52, no. 1 (October 2007): 71–84. https://doi.org/10.1002/j.2161-007x.2007.tb00088.x.

Schaefer, Natascha, Carola Rotermund, Eva-Maria Blumrich, Mychael V. Lourenco, Pooja Joshi, Regina U. Hegemann, Sumit Jamwal, et al. "The Malleable Brain: Plasticity of Neural Circuits and Behavior - a Review from Students to Students." *Journal of Neurochemistry* 142, no. 6 (August 8, 2017): 790–811. https://doi.org/10.1111/jnc.14107.

Schlatter, Marc G, Long V Nguyen, Maria Tecos, Elle L Kalbfell, Omar Gonzalez-Vega, and Tedi Vlahu. "Progressive Reduction of Hospital Length of Stay Following Minimally Invasive Repair of Pectus Excavatum: A Retrospective Comparison of Three Analgesia Modalities, the Role of Addressing Patient Anxiety, and Reframing Patient Expectations." *Journal of Pediatric Surgery* 54, no. 4 (April 2019): 663–69. https://doi.org/10.1016/j.jpedsurg.2018.12.003.

Schreiner, Istvan, and James P. Malcolm. "The Benefits of Mindfulness Meditation: Changes in Emotional States of Depression, Anxiety, and Stress." *Behaviour Change* 25, no. 3 (September 1, 2008): 156–68. https://doi.org/10.1375/bech.25.3.156.

Schwartz, Jeffrey M., and Sharon Begley. *The Mind and the Brain: Neuroplasticity and the Power of Mental Force.* New York: Regan Books/Harper Collins Publishers, 2002.

Siddall, Philip J., Melanie Lovell, and Rod MacLeod. "Spirituality: What Is Its Role in Pain Medicine?" *Pain Medicine* 16, no. 1 (January 2015): 51–60. https://doi.org/10.1111/pme.12511.

Sood, Sumeet, S. S. Chandla, Ravi Kant Dogra, Saumya Das, S. K. Shukla, and Sanjay Gupta. "Effect of Short-Term Practice of Pranayamic Breathing Exercises on Cognition, Anxiety, General Well Being and Heart Rate Variability." *Journal of the Indian Medical Association* 111, no. 10 (October 2013): 662–65.

Swinburne, Richard. *The Existence of God.* Oxford, England: Oxford University Press on Demand, 2004.

Williams, Joshua A., David Meltzer, Vineet Arora, Grace Chung, and Farr A. Curlin. "Attention to Inpatients' Religious and Spiritual Concerns: Predictors and Association with Patient Satisfaction." *Journal of General Internal Medicine* 26, no. 11 (July 1, 2011): 1265–71. https://doi.org/10.1007/s11606-011-1781-y.

Zeidan, Fadel, Susan K. Johnson, Bruce J. Diamond, Zhanna David, and Paula Goolkasian. "Mindfulness Meditation Improves Cognition: Evidence of Brief Mental Training." *Consciousness and Cognition* 19, no. 2 (June 2010): 597–605. https://doi.org/10.1016/j.concog.2010.03.014.

Acknowledgements

To my loving Parents:

A spiritual guru once told me that we choose who we want as parents before we come into this world. My soul knew the lessons I needed to learn and the experiences that would help me become the person I was intended to be. I chose you both. You have been and continue to be the perfect parents for me. You have given me everything I needed to bring me to this moment. My appreciation, love, and gratitude are without bounds.

Elyse:

My sweet daughter, you are the greatest treasure I have ever been given. I love you all the time.

Gilbert:

Thank you for allowing me to be me, loving me and supporting me along the way. I love, respect, and adore you.

Doug:

Wherever this journey of life takes us, I hope we continue to travel the same path.

Amy Tewes:

I'm not sure I would be where I am without your friendship, knowledge, and support. You have been a shining light leading me and guiding me in this entire process.

Matthew Gilbert:

It was such a pleasure collaborating with you. Thank you for seeing my vision and believing in me. You have inspired me to make my words my art and allow my truths to flow.

Stacy and Nitzia of Stacy Burk Photography:

Thank you for sharing your beautiful energy, love of nature and adventure, and extraordinary talent. The photographs that you captured encompass The Conqueress so powerfully.

Doug MacLeod and Keith Maginn:

Thank you for your support and expertise throughout this entire process.

Susan Linder and Suzanne Cook:

Your wisdom, love, and support helped me recover from the darkness of the Fall and step into the light. I love you always.

About the Author

Dr. Marcy B. PhD, is a Health Psychologist with a passion to help others unlock their inner self. She also holds a graduate degree in Educational Psychology, plus over a decade of experience working in the field. Dr. Marcy B is a certified Trauma Professional and MBSR (Mindful-Based Stress Reduction) Instructor. With degrees and certifications, she still found herself grinding through her own personal, life-altering hardships. During the worst stress, she came face-to-face with jarring truths about her own identity, and unpacked dysfunctional patterns in her life. She broke through. She found her inner Conqueress. It was an epiphany: her life's calling was to decode and synthesize her years of institutional schooling, professional experience, and personal 'ah-ha's' and serve it to others in a practical and empowering way. Dr. Marcy B.'s tools offer tangible steps toward cultivating your inborn purpose of existence in a thriving manner. Her happy place is anywhere she can feel the sun on her skin, hear her daughter's laughter and witness breakthroughs instead of breakdowns. She offers *The Conqueress* -- the innate power to transform your life. She'd love to follow your transformation as you read this book; post your journey at @drmarcyb on Facebook or @dr.marcyb on Instagram.

CPSIA information can be obtained
at www.ICGtesting.com
Printed in the USA
LVHW092128250621
691050LV00011B/228

9 781982 267438